The Resilient Entrepreneur

Navigating Failure to Find Success

BY

OLADEJI AFOLABI

Copyright © 2024

Oladeji Afolabi

ALL RIGHTS RESERVED

No part of this book may be reproduced, distributed, or transmitted in any form or by any means without the prior written permission of the publisher, except in the case of brief quotations embodied in critical reviews and certain other noncommercial uses permitted by copyright law.

Table of Contents

Author's Note..6
The Resilient Entrepreneur..7
The Spark of Entrepreneurship..4
    From Employee to Entrepreneur...4
    Identifying the Right Opportunity..7
    Overcoming Self-Doubt..9
    Building a Support Network..12
    Taking the Leap: From Idea to Action....................................14
The Pitfalls and Perseverance...18
    Learning From Failure 18
    Financial Crises: From Bust to Bankruptcy 21
    Balancing Work and Personal Life 24
    Dealing With Competition 27
    The Power of Perseverance 29
Reinvention and Innovation..31
    Embracing Change and Adaptability 31
    Harnessing the Power of Innovation 34
    Disruptive Technologies and Trends 37
    Continuous Learning and Personal Growth 40
    Reinventing the Entrepreneurial Identity 42
Lessons Learned...45
    Lessons and Insights 45
    Broader Principles 47
Leadership and Team Building...50

- The Qualities of Effective Leaders 50
- Building and Managing High-Performing Teams 52
- The Art of Delegation 55
- Conflict Resolution and Collaboration 57
- Cultivating a Positive Work Culture 62

Strategic Planning and Execution.. 65
- Setting SMART Goals 65
- Creating a Strategic Business Plan 68
- Effective Implementation and Execution 71
- Risk Management and Contingency Planning 73
- Evaluating and Adjusting Strategies 76

Marketing and Branding... 80
- Understanding Target Audiences 80
- Crafting Compelling Marketing Messages 84
- Building a Strong Brand Identity 86
- Effective Online Marketing Strategies 89
- Building Customer Relationships and Loyalty 91

Financial Management and Growth... 95
- Financial Planning and Budgeting 95
- Funding Options for Entrepreneurs 98
- Managing Business Finances 100
- Strategies for Sustainable Growth 103
- Financial Metrics and Performance Evaluation 106

Rising Strong:... 110
From Starting To Finishing Strong.. 110

Author's Note

Welcome to "The Resilient Entrepreneur." I am deeply grateful for your decision to join me on this transformative journey through the ups and downs of entrepreneurship. Crafting this book has been a passionate endeavor, driven by the firm belief that setbacks are not roadblocks but rather opportunities for growth and resilience.

Within the pages that follow, you'll encounter a wealth of insights, strategies, and real-life narratives from individuals who have faced adversity head-on and emerged triumphant. This book serves as a guiding light for those navigating the often turbulent waters of business, offering a roadmap from hardship to triumph.

I encourage you to immerse yourself in these pages, allowing the stories and lessons shared to resonate with your own experiences. Your feedback is invaluable to me. Whether you discover new found inspiration, glean insightful perspectives, or identify areas where we can collectively improve, I urge you to share your thoughts. Your reviews not only shape my understanding but also contribute to the broader wisdom of our entrepreneurial community.

Thank you for embarking on this journey with me.

Warm regards,

Oladeji Afolabi

The Resilient Entrepreneur

INTRODUCTION

Imagine a young entrepreneur, their dreams slipping through their fingers like grains of sand. The weight of failure pressing down on their weary shoulders as they contemplate their next move. But instead of succumbing to despair, they rise from the ashes, like a phoenix soaring through the skies. With sheer tenacity and unwavering grit, they transform their failures into stepping stones, paving the way for unimaginable success.

The kind of story that leaves you on the edge of your seat, your heart pounding, and a renewed sense of hope flooding through every fiber of your being? Well, let me tell you – the tale I am about to share with you is just like that. But make no mistake, this is not a fictional story spun from the depths of my imagination. No, this is a true account, a collection of remarkable narratives from the lives of entrepreneurs who have experienced the tumultuous rollercoaster of success and failure, including myself.

Join me on a journey through "The Resilient Entrepreneur," as we delve deep into the lives of these brave souls who have navigated the treacherous waters of the business world.

Each chapter in this book is an invitation to explore a different entrepreneur's redemption story. From the ashes of their failed ventures, they have risen, stronger and wiser than ever before. You will uncover not only their business strategies and innovative ideas but also the personal growth and transformation that came hand-in-hand with their entrepreneurial journeys.

Here, you will walk side by side with these extraordinary individuals as they navigate the stormy seas of uncertainty. You will witness their hopes crumble, their dreams shattered, and their spirits tested. But fear not, for this is not a tale of despair or sorrow. On the contrary, it is a testament to the resilience and indomitable spirit of the human soul.

As you turn each page, you will find yourself captivated by the raw emotions and sheer determination that emanate from these stories. You will feel their triumphs reverberate through your veins, and their failures will serve as cautionary tales, guiding you away from the pitfalls that lie in wait.

So, my dear reader, whether you are an aspiring entrepreneur yearning for guidance, a driven individual seeking inspiration, or simply a curious soul hungry for captivating tales, this book is for you. Within these pages, you will find answers to the questions that haunt your restless mind. You will discover that redemption is not just a distant dream but a tangible reality within your grasp.

Prepare to be moved, to be inspired, and to be captivated by the tales of these extraordinary entrepreneurs. Let their stories serve as a beacon of light in the darkest of times, igniting a fire within you that can never be extinguished.

This is not just a book; it is an invitation to embark on a transformational journey. So, are you ready to join me on this extraordinary adventure through "The Resilient Entrepreneur"? Let the redemption begin.

Chapter One
The Spark of Entrepreneurship

A visionary like Elon Musk, fueled by a passion for sustainable transportation, co-founded Tesla. Musk's dedication to hastening the world's adoption of electric vehicles sparks an automotive revolution. Under his leadership, Tesla's innovative approach not only challenges conventional norms but reshapes the future of transportation as we know it.

From Employee to Entrepreneur

As I reflect on my journey from employee to entrepreneur, I vividly recall the mix of excitement and apprehension that accompanied my decision to leave the security of my job and venture into the unpredictable world of entrepreneurship. This transition demanded a profound shift in mindset, a leap into uncharted territory, and an unwavering commitment to confront the challenges that lay ahead.

One of the primary hurdles I encountered during this transition was the fear of failure. As an employee, I had grown accustomed to a stable income, predictable working hours, and the comfort of knowing that someone else bore the majority of business responsibilities. Yet, as an entrepreneur, the weight of success or failure rested squarely on my shoulders. The anxiety of not succeeding, of potentially squandering time, money, and effort, cast a heavy shadow.

To combat this fear, I had to embrace a new perspective. I reminded myself that failure is an inherent part of the entrepreneurial journey. It is through these trials, the lessons from missteps, that success ultimately emerges. I sought inspiration from the experiences of seasoned entrepreneurs who had weathered their share of setbacks before achieving remarkable success. Their stories served as a wellspring of encouragement, reminding me that failure wasn't a dead end but a stepping stone toward triumph.

Another challenge that surfaced during this transition was the uncertainty of income. As an employee, I received regular paychecks on a fixed schedule. However, as an entrepreneur, my income was inextricably tied to the fate of my business. This meant adapting to a life of financial instability and mastering the ebbs and flows of entrepreneurship.

To mitigate this uncertainty, I undertook careful financial planning and budgeting. I assessed my expenses, considered potential revenue sources, and set realistic financial objectives. I embraced the concept of living within my means, understanding that sacrifices might be necessary during the early stages of my entrepreneurial voyage. By adopting a prudent and strategic approach to financial management, I was able to alleviate some of the anxiety related to income unpredictability.

The transition from employee to entrepreneur also ushered in a new set of responsibilities and challenges. No longer could I depend on colleagues or superiors to make decisions or solve problems. Every facet of my business, from the grand vision to the minute details of execution, rested solely on my shoulders. This newfound autonomy was both liberating and overwhelming.

To navigate this uncharted terrain, I sought counsel from mentors and engaged with entrepreneurial communities. These networks provided invaluable support, offering a community of like-minded individuals grappling with similar challenges. Through shared experiences, advice, and collaborative ventures, I tapped into a wealth of knowledge that aided me in navigating the intricacies of entrepreneurship.

The challenges I confronted throughout this transition were indeed formidable, yet they forged me into a more resilient and resourceful entrepreneur. Rather than regarding them as insurmountable obstacles, I learned to see them as opportunities for growth and development. Each hurdle I faced served as a lesson, a chance to refine my skills and enhance my business.

To thrive as an entrepreneur, I recognized the significance of continual learning and evolution. I immersed myself in books, podcasts, and online courses pertaining to entrepreneurship, leadership, and personal development. I participated in workshops and conferences, actively seeking opportunities to gain fresh perspectives and connect with industry leaders. I also valued feedback from clients and customers, constantly striving to enhance my products and services.

The journey from employee to entrepreneur is undeniably challenging and uncertain. It demands a shift in mindset, a readiness to embrace failure, and the ability to adapt to the uncertainties and responsibilities inherent in running a business. Nevertheless, by seeking guidance, planning meticulously, and perpetually learning and evolving, the path from employee to entrepreneur can be an enriching and transformative experience.

Identifying the Right Opportunity

As an entrepreneur, I have learned the hard way that not all opportunities are created equal. There have been times when I jumped into a business venture without proper research and ended up paying a hefty price for my impulsive decisions. But through these failures, I have honed my skills of identifying the right opportunity, and now, I am here to share my insights with you.

Market research is the backbone of any successful business endeavor. It lays the foundation for understanding the target market, competition, and customer needs. It involves collecting and analyzing data related to your industry, consumer behavior, and market trends. This information is vital in shaping your business strategies and determining the potential success of your venture.

When I was first starting out, I neglected the importance of thorough market research. I thought I had a brilliant idea and rushed into launching my business without conducting proper analysis. It was a disaster. I soon realized that my target market was saturated, and there was no room for a new player. I failed to understand the needs and preferences of my potential customers, and as a result, my product was a complete mismatch. I learned from this failure and vowed never to make the same mistake again.

Trend analysis is another crucial aspect of identifying the right opportunity. It involves studying the current and emerging trends in your industry. By staying ahead of the curve, you can tap into the market demand and position yourself as an innovative and relevant player.

In today's fast-paced world, trends come and go rapidly. Just think about how quickly social media platforms have evolved over the years. If you want to stay in the game, you need to embrace change and adapt your business accordingly. Trend analysis allows you to anticipate shifts in consumer preferences and adjust your strategy accordingly. Whether it's a new technology, a change in consumer behavior, or a growing market segment, staying abreast of trends can open doors to new and promising business opportunities.

Let me share a personal example. A few years ago, I noticed a growing trend of health and fitness among millennials. Gym memberships were skyrocketing, healthy eating was becoming a lifestyle choice, and people were constantly seeking ways to improve their overall well-being.

This trend sparked an idea in my mind. I decided to dive deeper into the health and wellness industry and explore potential opportunities within this niche. Through extensive research, I found a gap in the market for customizable meal delivery services. I seized the opportunity and launched a successful business that catered to health-conscious individuals seeking convenient and nutritious meals. By identifying and capitalizing on a popular trend, I was able to position myself as a leader in this niche market.

Finding a niche is a vital step in identifying the right opportunity. It involves identifying a specific segment within your industry that is underserved or overlooked. By focusing on a niche, you can differentiate yourself from the competition and establish a loyal customer base.

When I was struggling to find success as an entrepreneur, I decided to take a step back and reassess my approach. That's when I stumbled upon the concept of niche marketing. I realized that my previous ventures failed because I was trying to cater to a broad market without specializing in anything specific. I needed to find a niche that aligned with my passion and expertise. After careful consideration, I discovered my passion for eco-friendly products and realized there was a growing demand for sustainable alternatives in the market. Armed with this knowledge, I started a business that focused on providing eco-friendly household products. By targeting a specific audience and addressing their unique needs, my business thrived and became a recognized brand in the market.

Identifying the right opportunity is not an easy task. It requires time, research, and a keen sense of observation. But by conducting thorough market research, analyzing trends, and finding a niche, you can significantly increase your chances of success as an entrepreneur. So, before you dive headfirst into a new business venture, take a step back, assess the market, and choose the path that will lead you to entrepreneurial redemption. Remember, the right opportunity is out there - you just have to find it.

Overcoming Self-Doubt

Throughout my journey as an entrepreneur, I have encountered moments of crippling self-doubt. The nagging voice in my head questioning my abilities and competence has often threatened to derail my aspirations. It was not until I discovered the strategies and techniques outlined in this subchapter that I was able to overcome these internal barriers and build unwavering confidence in myself.

Self-doubt is often a natural phenomenon that plagues even the most successful individuals. It stems from a deep-rooted fear of failure and a lack of faith in one's skills and capabilities. As aspiring entrepreneurs, we are often stepping into uncharted territories, taking risks, and venturing into the unknown. This can be a breeding ground for self-doubt to flourish.

Imposter syndrome, a variant of self-doubt, adds an additional layer of complexity to the entrepreneurial journey. It is characterized by the persistent feeling of being a fraud, despite evidence of one's accomplishments. Imposter syndrome can be particularly detrimental to an entrepreneur's confidence and success, as it undermines their self-belief and ability to capitalize on opportunities.

Addressing self-doubt and imposter syndrome requires a multi-faceted approach. The first step is to acknowledge and accept these feelings as normal. It is crucial to understand that self-doubt is a part of the human condition and does not define our worth or potential. By acknowledging its presence, we can take proactive steps to counter its effect on our entrepreneurial journey.

One of the most effective strategies to overcome self-doubt is by focusing on our strengths and past accomplishments. Often, our self-doubt blinds us to the progress we have made and the skills we have developed along the way. Reflecting on our achievements, no matter how small, can serve as a powerful reminder of our capabilities and instill a sense of belief in our entrepreneurial prowess. Keeping a journal of our successes and revisiting it during moments of self-doubt can provide a much-needed boost of confidence.

Cultivating a growth mindset is another essential component of overcoming self-doubt. Embracing the belief that we have the capacity to learn and grow allows us to view setbacks and failures as opportunities for improvement rather than evidence of our incompetence. By reframing our mindset, we can transform self-doubt into a catalyst for growth and development. It is a shift from "I can't do this" to "I can learn and improve."

Seeking support from mentors, peers, and fellow entrepreneurs can be instrumental in combating self-doubt. Surrounding ourselves with a network of individuals who believe in our potential and provide constructive feedback can offer reassurance during moments of uncertainty. Engaging in open and honest conversations about our fears and insecurities with trusted individuals helps to normalize the experience of self-doubt and reminds us that we are not alone in this journey.

Developing a routine of self-care and self-compassion is vital in building resilience in the face of self-doubt. Entrepreneurship can be an arduous and demanding path, and it is crucial to prioritize our mental and emotional well-being. Taking time to nurture ourselves through activities that bring us joy and relaxation can recharge our confidence and energy levels. Practicing self-compassion by treating ourselves with kindness and understanding during moments of self-doubt prevents us from succumbing to negative self-talk and self-sabotage.

Taking calculated risks is an integral part of entrepreneurship. However, self-doubt often paralyzes our ability to make decisions and seize opportunities. Developing a habit of setting small, achievable goals and gradually expanding our comfort zone enables us to build confidence in our decision-making abilities. Each successful step towards our goals reinforces our belief in ourselves and diminishes the power of self-doubt.

Lastly, embracing failure as a learning opportunity is key to overcoming self-doubt. Failure is an inevitable part of the entrepreneurial journey, and it is essential to reframe our perspective on failure. Instead of viewing it as a personal inadequacy, we should view it as a stepping stone towards success. Each failure provides valuable lessons and insights that can fuel our growth and guide us towards future accomplishments. By reframing our perspective on failure, we can neutralize the paralyzing effect of self-doubt and transform it into a motivating force.

In conclusion, self-doubt and imposter syndrome are common obstacles faced by aspiring entrepreneurs. However, by employing these strategies and techniques, we can overcome these internal barriers and build unwavering confidence in our abilities. The path to entrepreneurship is not without challenges, but by addressing and combating self-doubt, we can unlock our full potential and achieve greatness.

Building a Support Network

When I first embarked on my entrepreneurial journey, I was overwhelmed by the challenges and uncertainties that lay ahead. I had a vision and a passion for my business, but I lacked the experience and knowledge to navigate the complex world of entrepreneurship. It was at this critical juncture that I realized the significance of surrounding myself with individuals who had already been through the trenches and emerged victorious.

I began by seeking out mentors—those who had achieved success in similar industries or possessed the skills and expertise I aspired to acquire. These mentors became not only a source of guidance but also a source of inspiration and motivation. They shared their experiences, the ups and downs of their entrepreneurial journeys, and provided valuable insights into overcoming obstacles. I truly believe that without their wisdom and support, I would not have been able to weather the storm and eventually thrive.

In addition to mentors, I also actively sought out advisors who could provide specific expertise in areas where I lacked knowledge. I recognized that I couldn't excel at everything and that seeking help from others who had mastered those skills was not a sign of weakness, but rather a demonstration of my commitment to growth. These advisors became my trusted allies in areas such as finance, marketing, and product development. Their insights and feedback enabled me to make informed decisions and avoid costly mistakes.

I remember a particular scenario when I was struggling with my first business, which was a software company, I had coffee time with one of my mentors, who is an architect and has several businesses including four hotels, a real estate firm, and an architectural firm. He made me understand the place of differentiating "professionalism" from "entrepreneurship". He made me see for the first time that I was still thinking like a professional rather than an entrepreneur. The words sank in. The difference was understood, literally. But the paradigm shift took a while. Without a mentor at that point, I probably would take much longer to understand and put that to use.

However, building a support network goes beyond mentorship and advisory relationships. It also involves connecting and collaborating with other entrepreneurs who share similar ambitions and values. Networking became a vital aspect of my journey, as it allowed me to expand my horizons, learn from others' experiences, and gain exposure to new opportunities. By attending industry events, workshops, and conferences, I was able to establish meaningful connections with like-minded individuals who understood the challenges and joys of entrepreneurship.

Collaboration within my support network became the driving force behind my success. I quickly learned that we are stronger together than we are alone. Through collaboration, we were able to leverage each other's strengths, pool resources, and collectively tackle obstacles that would have been insurmountable as individuals. The power of collaboration lies not only in the shared knowledge and expertise but also in the emotional support and camaraderie it provides. Being able to share both successes and failures with others who understand the entrepreneurial journey on a deeply personal level has been instrumental in keeping me motivated and resilient.

Entrepreneurship can be a lonely road at times, and seeking guidance from experienced entrepreneurs who have been in your shoes is invaluable. These seasoned entrepreneurs have faced the same challenges, made their fair share of mistakes, and come out stronger on the other side. They can offer practical advice, guidance, and even serve as role models, providing the inspiration needed to push through the toughest of times. I found myself fortunate to have crossed paths with several of these individuals who generously shared their wisdom, supported me during setbacks, and celebrated my victories.

As I reflect on the impact of building a support network, I realize that it extends beyond individual success. It fosters a sense of community and collaboration within the entrepreneurial ecosystem, leading to a collective upliftment. When entrepreneurs come together to support and uplift each other, amazing things can happen. New ideas are born, partnerships are formed, and opportunities multiply.

In essence, building a strong support network is not merely a luxury for entrepreneurs but an essential part of their journey toward redemption. Surrounding oneself with mentors, advisors, and like-minded individuals brings valuable guidance, expertise, and emotional support. Collaboration and networking opportunities further enhance the potential for growth and success. By seeking out the wisdom of experienced entrepreneurs, we can learn from their triumphs and failures, gaining insights into navigating the treacherous waters of entrepreneurship. No entrepreneur can embark on this journey alone; it is the strength of our support network that propels us forward, bringing us closer to our goals and ultimately our own redemption.

Taking the Leap: From Idea to Action

As an entrepreneur, I have come to realize that having a great idea is just the beginning. It is the spark that ignites the fire of passion and motivation within us. But in order to turn that idea into a successful venture, there are crucial steps that need to be taken. This section, "Taking the Leap: From Idea to Action," serves as a guide for readers who are eager to transform their entrepreneurial ideas into actionable plans.

Setting goals is the first step on this journey. Without clear and attainable goals, our ideas may remain elusive dreams. Therefore, it is vital to define what we ultimately aim to achieve and outline the steps required to get there. Setting goals creates a sense of direction and acts as a roadmap to success. It helps us stay focused amidst the inevitable challenges we will encounter along the way.

In my own entrepreneurial journey, I learned the importance of creating a business plan. A well-structured business plan serves as a blueprint for our ideas, outlining the strategies and tactics necessary for bringing them to life. It not only helps us clarify our vision but also provides a roadmap for potential investors or partners who may be interested in joining our venture. It is a document that encapsulates our mission, target market, competitive analysis, marketing strategies, financial projections, and more.

To create an effective business plan, we must conduct thorough research. Understanding our target market, analyzing competitors, and identifying trends are essential components of this process. By delving into the needs and desires of our potential customers, we can identify gaps in the market and tailor our offerings accordingly. Furthermore, researching competitors can help us differentiate ourselves and position our business uniquely. Successful entrepreneurs know that knowledge is power, and a well-researched business plan is a powerful tool.

Once our goals are set and our business plan is in place, it is time to take action. This is where the rubber meets the road. It is easy to get caught up in the excitement of generating ideas and brainstorming strategies, but without implementation, they remain mere fantasies. The process of taking action involves breaking down our larger goals into smaller, actionable steps. By setting milestones and deadlines, we can ensure progress and avoid feeling overwhelmed. Each small step taken in the right direction brings us closer to accomplishing our ultimate vision.

However, taking action requires determination and resilience. There will be setbacks and obstacles along the way, but it is important to remain adaptable and persistent. As I embarked on my entrepreneurial journey, I had to confront numerous challenges, from securing funding to establishing a strong team. I quickly realized that success is not a linear path but rather a series of ups and downs. It is the ability to learn from failures, adapt our strategies, and keep pushing forward that sets successful entrepreneurs apart.

Building a network of support is also crucial during this phase. Surrounding ourselves with like-minded individuals who share our passion and enthusiasm can provide the motivation and guidance we need. Whether it is seeking advice from mentors, connecting with fellow entrepreneurs, or attending industry events, building relationships is key. These connections can open doors to new opportunities and provide valuable insights from those who have already walked the path we aspire to tread.

In addition to our network, continuous learning is essential. The entrepreneurial ecosystem is dynamic and constantly evolving. Staying updated on industry trends, emerging technologies, and best practices is vital for staying ahead of the competition. Engaging in online courses, attending workshops, and reading industry publications can equip us with the knowledge and skills necessary to navigate the ever-changing landscape.

Taking the leap from idea to action is a transformative experience. It requires courage, determination, and a relentless passion for our vision. Each step we take brings us closer to our dreams, but it is the collective effort of setting goals, creating a business plan, conducting thorough research, and taking action that propels us toward success. As we embark on this journey, let us embrace the challenges and possibilities that lie ahead, knowing that the rewards of entrepreneurship are within our reach.

As I reflect on my own journey, I am reminded of the countless nights spent fine-tuning my business setup documents (business plan, agreements templates, vision/mission statements, and marketing/sales strategy), the sacrifices made, and the relentless pursuit of my dreams. It is through taking action that I have seen my idea come to life, my business flourish, and my entrepreneurial spirit soar. Now, it is time for you, dear reader, to take the leap and turn your entrepreneurial ideas into actionable plans. Embrace the challenges, fuel your determination, and let your dreams become your reality.

Chapter Two
The Pitfalls and Perseverance

Oprah Winfrey's journey to media mogul status was far from a smooth ascent. She faced adversity throughout her early career but persevered with unwavering determination. Her path serves as a testament to resilience, demonstrating how she rose above adversity to become one of the most influential figures in media and entertainment.

Learning From Failure

Failure. The very word holds a weight that can make even the strongest of us shudder. It conjures up images of disappointment, regret, and a sense of defeat. We are raised in a society that teaches us to fear failure and avoid it at all costs. But what if failure was not our enemy? What if, instead, it was our greatest ally in the pursuit of success?

Throughout my entrepreneurial journey, I have faced countless failures. From the moment I started my first business to the present day, failure has been a constant companion. Truth be told, it is overwhelming and horrible to experience. But rather than allowing it to consume me, I have learned to see failure as a valuable teacher. It has taught me more about myself, my abilities, and my business than any success ever could.

Embracing failure is not an easy task. It requires a shift in mindset, a willingness to let go of pride and ego, and a deep understanding that failure does not define us. It is merely a part of the journey towards success. The first step in embracing failure is to redefine what it means to us. Rather than seeing failure as the end, we must see it as a stepping stone towards future success.

Failure is not a destination, but rather a detour on the road to success. Each failure brings with it valuable lessons and opportunities for growth. It is in those moments of defeat that we are forced to confront our weaknesses, analyze our mistakes, and find new ways to move forward. Without failure, we would never truly understand the true measure of our abilities.

Analyzing our failures is a crucial step in the learning process. It requires a willingness to be honest with ourselves, to acknowledge our mistakes, and to learn from them. This self-reflection is not always easy or comfortable, but it is necessary if we are to grow and improve. By analyzing our failures, we can identify patterns, uncover weaknesses, and develop strategies to overcome them. It is through this process of self-reflection that we can turn failure into a valuable learning opportunity.

But analyzing our failures alone is not enough. We must also learn to use them as stepping stones towards future success. Each failure presents us with a unique opportunity to grow, adapt, and evolve. It forces us to challenge our assumptions, explore new perspectives, and develop innovative solutions. By embracing failure and using it as a catalyst for change, we can transform our setbacks into stepping stones toward future success.

One of the greatest entrepreneurs of our time, Thomas Edison, famously said, "I have not failed. I've just found 10,000 ways that won't work." His relentless pursuit of success and his ability to embrace failure as a valuable teacher is what ultimately led him to invent the light bulb. Edison understood that failure was not an obstacle, but rather a necessary part of the creative process. It was through his failures that he learned what did not work, and in doing so, he brought himself one step closer to what would work.

In my own entrepreneurial journey, failure has been both my greatest adversary and my greatest ally. It has taught me humility, resilience, and the importance of perseverance. It has forced me to confront my weaknesses head-on, question my assumptions, and continually adapt and evolve. Each failure I have experienced has made me stronger, more resilient, and more determined to succeed.

One of the harshest experiences of failures I experienced was, I went to another country to open a new business while the parent business was still running in my home country. In the new location, opportunities came in rapidly and so did my yearning for expansion. I poured every available fund into full expansion in this new country, which I had barely established for 18 months. I unconsciously neglected the parent business back home to the full judgment of employed managers. I was badly burnt because of this premature growth. All funds invested were lost. Time was wasted. The parent business was affected terribly. I was personally devastated. I lost balance, even psychologically, for about a year, but remembering I had to use the failure as a tool for improvement, I reset and it became an invaluable lesson.

Failure is not the end. It is merely a stepping stone towards future success. By embracing failure, analyzing our mistakes, and using them as opportunities for growth, we can transform our setbacks into stepping stones toward our ultimate goals. It is through failure that we truly learn, grow, and evolve as entrepreneurs. So, the next time you face failure, embrace it. Learn from it. And use it as a springboard toward your own redemption.

Financial Crises: From Bust to Bankruptcy

One of the most common financial challenges entrepreneurs face is managing cash flow. Cash flow is the lifeblood of any business, and without it, even the most promising ventures can crumble. In order to effectively manage cash flow, entrepreneurs must have a deep understanding of their business's financial health and project their future cash inflows and outflows. This requires maintaining accurate financial records and regularly monitoring and analyzing the company's financial statements.

To minimize the risk of cash flow difficulties, entrepreneurs should consider implementing various strategies. One such strategy is to negotiate favorable payment terms with suppliers and customers. By extending payment terms with suppliers and tightening credit terms with customers, entrepreneurs can ensure a continuous inflow of cash while giving themselves some breathing room. Additionally, entrepreneurs should actively manage their working capital, including inventory levels, accounts receivable, and accounts payable, to optimize the flow of cash within the business.

My experience, as detailed earlier, underscores the vital importance of prudent cash flow management. Neglecting the financial health of my original business while pursuing rapid expansion in a new country had severe consequences. It serves as a real-life lesson in the need for a balanced approach to growth opportunities and the critical role of sound cash flow management in sustaining and growing a business.

Securing funding is another significant challenge entrepreneurs often face. Whether it is to fund a new project, expand operations, or ride out a financial downturn, entrepreneurs need access to capital. However, obtaining funding can be a daunting task, as banks and investors are often skeptical of small and emerging businesses. In such situations, entrepreneurs must be resourceful and explore alternative options for funding.

One alternative option for funding is bootstrapping. Bootstrapping refers to building and growing a business with minimal external capital. This can be achieved by reinvesting profits back into the business, carefully managing expenses, and seeking creative ways to generate revenue. While bootstrapping may require entrepreneurs to start small and grow slowly, it can also provide them with greater control over their business and its finances.

For entrepreneurs in need of substantial capital, seeking out external investors or securing a business loan are potential options. When approaching investors, entrepreneurs should be prepared with a compelling business plan, a solid track record, and a clear vision for the future. Investors want to see that their money will be put to good use and that there is a high likelihood of a return on investment. Similarly, when applying for a business loan, entrepreneurs need to present their financial statements, demonstrate their ability to repay the loan, and explain how the funds will be utilized to grow the business.

Even with proper cash flow management and funding in place, entrepreneurs may still find themselves navigating through difficult financial situations. Economic downturns, unexpected events, or industry disruptions can severely impact a business's finances and push it to the brink of bankruptcy. In these situations, swift action and strategic decision-making are crucial to secure the business's survival.

One possible strategy for navigating through difficult financial situations is cost-cutting. Entrepreneurs should analyze their operating expenses and identify areas where costs can be reduced without compromising the quality of their products or services. This may involve renegotiating contracts with suppliers, implementing efficiency measures in production processes, or exploring alternative suppliers or vendors.

Another strategy is diversifying revenue streams. Relying heavily on a single product, service, or customer can leave a business susceptible to financial shocks. By diversifying their offerings and customer base, entrepreneurs can spread the risk and ensure a more stable income stream. This may involve expanding into new markets, introducing new products or services, or targeting new customer segments.

Entrepreneurs facing financial crises should also consider seeking professional advice. Hiring a financial consultant or working with a business turnaround specialist can provide valuable insights and guidance in developing a comprehensive recovery plan. These experts can help entrepreneurs identify the root causes of their financial challenges, implement necessary changes, and devise strategies to restore profitability and sustainable growth.

In times of financial crises, it is crucial for entrepreneurs to stay focused, adaptable, and resilient. While the road to redemption may be challenging and uncertain, with the right strategies and mindset, entrepreneurs can turn their businesses around, emerge stronger, and achieve long-term success. By managing cash flow effectively, securing funding, and navigating through difficult financial situations, entrepreneurs can write a new chapter in their entrepreneurial journey, one of resilience, growth, and redemption.

Balancing Work and Personal Life

I am a firm believer in the power of a healthy work-life balance. In the early days of my entrepreneurial journey, I made the mistake of neglecting my personal life in pursuit of success. I worked long hours, sacrificed sleep and social interactions, and ultimately burned out. It was a harsh wake-up call that taught me the importance of finding an equilibrium between work and personal life.

Extensive research has shown that maintaining a healthy work-life balance leads to increased productivity, better mental health, and overall satisfaction in life. Taking time to recharge and engage in activities that bring joy and fulfillment outside of work is crucial for maintaining long-term success as an entrepreneur.

Tips for Balancing Work and Personal Life

Now that we understand the significance of work-life balance, let's delve into some practical tips and techniques to help you achieve it.

1. ***Prioritize Self-Care***
   Putting self-care at the forefront of your life is essential for maintaining balance. Make sure to schedule time for activities that recharge your batteries, such as exercise, meditation, or pursuing hobbies. Remember, taking care of yourself is not a luxury; it is a necessity.

2. ***Set Boundaries***
   Establishing boundaries is crucial for preventing work from bleeding into personal life. Clearly define your working hours and communicate them to your team, clients, and loved ones. This way,

you can protect personal time and establish a clear line between work and leisure.

3. *Delegate and Automate*

One of the secrets to maintaining a healthy work-life balance is learning to delegate and automate tasks. As an entrepreneur, it can be tempting to take on every responsibility yourself, but this can quickly lead to burnout. Identify tasks that can be delegated or automated, freeing up valuable time for more personally fulfilling activities.

4. *Find Support*

Entrepreneurship can be a lonely journey, but that doesn't mean you have to go it alone. Surround yourself with a supportive network of friends, family, and fellow entrepreneurs who understand the challenges you face. Seek advice, vent frustrations, and celebrate successes together. Remember, a problem shared is a problem halved.

5. *Practice Mindfulness*

Mindfulness is a powerful tool for cultivating balance and reducing stress. Incorporate mindfulness practices into your daily routine, such as meditation, deep breathing exercises, or simply taking a moment to pause and appreciate the present. Mindfulness helps you stay centered and present, regardless of the chaos happening around you.

6. *Embrace the Power of "No"*

Learning to say "no" is an art form that entrepreneurs must master. Saying "yes" to every opportunity or request that comes your way will only lead to overwhelm and exhaustion. Be selective in your commitments and learn to prioritize what aligns with your goals and values. Remember, every "no" opens the door to a more meaningful "yes."

7. **Schedule Personal Time**

Just as you schedule business meetings and appointments, it's crucial to schedule personal time. Block off time in your calendar for activities that bring you joy, whether it's spending time with loved ones, pursuing a hobby, or simply taking a well-deserved day off. Treat personal time as non-negotiable and guard it as you would a valuable business asset.

Continuing The Journey

Finding a healthy work-life balance is not a one-time event but an ongoing journey. As your business grows and evolves, so too will the demands on your time and energy. It's essential to regularly reassess and readjust your priorities to ensure you maintain equilibrium.

Remember, achieving work-life balance is not about achieving perfection but rather finding a sustainable rhythm that allows you to thrive both personally and professionally. By prioritizing self-care, setting boundaries, delegating, seeking support, practicing mindfulness, embracing the power of "no," and scheduling personal time, you can navigate the complexities of being an entrepreneur while maintaining a fulfilling personal life.

Remember, you hold the power to create the life you desire, one that allows you to not only achieve entrepreneurial success but also experience joy, fulfillment, and genuine connections outside of work.

Dealing With Competition

Competition in the business world is inevitable. As an entrepreneur, it is crucial to acknowledge and understand the competitive landscape in which you operate. The success or failure of your venture will largely depend on your ability to navigate through this fierce and unforgiving battleground. This section aims to equip you with the knowledge and strategies needed to not only survive but thrive in the face of competition.

The first step in dealing with competition is to differentiate yourself from your competitors. In a crowded marketplace, simply offering the same product or service as everyone else will not be enough to attract customers. You need to identify what makes your business unique and communicate that differentiation to your target audience.

For me, in the early days of my entrepreneurial journey, I faced the daunting task of standing out in the saturated tech industry. Though it was not as saturated as it is today, I found a niche in the neglected market for a start. My competition seemed to be offering similar products and services, and it was easy to get lost in the sea of options. However, through careful analysis and soul-searching, I discovered that my true strength lies in my ability to provide personalized customer experiences. I took time to research the specific "pains" of each prospect category. While other companies focused solely on the functionality of their software, I realized that I could gain a competitive edge by going above and beyond to understand and meet the individual needs of each of my clients.

Once you have identified your unique selling proposition, it is essential to constantly analyze and monitor your competitors. Understanding their strategies, strengths, and weaknesses will enable you to make informed decisions and anticipate market trends. This competitive intelligence will serve as a valuable tool in staying one step ahead.

I remember spending countless hours researching my competitors and dissecting their marketing campaigns. By doing so, I was able to identify gaps in the market and position my business as the go-to solution for customers who were dissatisfied with the offerings of my competitors. By leveraging these insights, I could tailor my messaging to highlight the areas in which I knew I had a competitive advantage.

However, analyzing competitors is not solely about finding weaknesses to exploit. It is also important to recognize their strengths and learn from their successes. By studying their strategies, I was able to gain inspiration and adapt them to fit my own business model. I created a culture within my team that encouraged innovation and learning from the best in the industry, both within and outside of our direct competition. This approach not only allowed us to stay current with the latest trends, but also ensured that we were continuously pushing the boundaries of what was possible in our field.

In addition to differentiation and competitor analysis, leveraging unique strengths is crucial in gaining a competitive edge. As an entrepreneur, you undoubtedly possess qualities and expertise that make you stand out from the crowd. Identifying and capitalizing on these strengths will set you apart and give you a distinct advantage in the marketplace.

For me, it was my ability to build strong relationships and foster a sense of trust and loyalty among my clients. While others may have had more technical expertise or a larger budget, the personal touch I brought to each client interaction allowed me to forge connections and secure long-term partnerships. This strength became the foundation of our reputation, and word-of-mouth referrals became one of our most effective marketing strategies.

It is important to remember that gaining a competitive edge is not a one-time achievement. The business landscape is ever-evolving, and what sets you apart today may not be sufficient tomorrow. It is essential to constantly reassess, adapt, and innovate to remain relevant and maintain your edge.

The competitive landscape can be intimidating for entrepreneurs, but by embracing it and implementing the strategies discussed so far, you can turn competition into an opportunity for growth. Differentiating yourself, analyzing competitors, and leveraging your unique strengths will not only help you gain a competitive edge, but also enable you to build a thriving and successful business. Embrace the challenge, stay nimble, and always be willing to evolve. In the words of Peter Drucker, "The entrepreneur always searches for change, responds to it, exploits it as an opportunity." Let competition be your catalyst for greatness.

The Power of Perseverance

As I sat down to write this, reflecting on the countless stories I've heard from entrepreneurs who have experienced both failure and success, one common theme emerged: perseverance. It is the driving force that separates those who give up when faced with difficulties from those who push forward, undeterred by setbacks. "Undeterred" doesn't imply that you won't be shaken or feel the intense pressure. "Perseverance" doesn't mean you won't experience moments when you contemplate quitting. Rather, it signifies a continuous process of resilience, a cycle of breaking and re-moulding oneself, often occurring behind the scenes, before any signs of setbacks become apparent.

Perseverance is not just a trait, but a mindset—a way of looking at challenges as opportunities for growth. It is the foundation upon which an entrepreneur's journey is built, providing the resilience needed to navigate the tumultuous waters of business. It is the unwavering determination that keeps us going when others would have thrown in the towel.

Let me share with you stories of renowned individuals whose life experiences vividly illustrate the practical power of perseverance. These are not just stories of success but real-life accounts of conquering adversity that can inspire and guide you.

1. ***Elon Musk's Unyielding Vision***
   Elon Musk, the visionary entrepreneur behind SpaceX and Tesla, faced numerous challenges and failures on his path to success. Musk famously said, 'Failure is an option here. If things are not failing, you are not innovating enough.' His relentless pursuit of transformative innovation, despite setbacks and skepticism, demonstrates the incredible potential of unwavering determination.

2. ***Oprah Winfrey's Rise Against All Odds***
   Oprah Winfrey, one of the most influential media moguls, overcame a challenging upbringing filled with poverty and abuse. Her perseverance in the face of adversity propelled her to become a global icon, showcasing the incredible potential of unwavering determination.

3. ***Steve Jobs' Resilient Vision***
   Steve Jobs, co-founder of Apple, was fired from his own company before making a triumphant return. His story epitomizes the spirit of perseverance, as he not only overcame personal setbacks but also reshaped the tech industry with his innovative vision.

These luminaries prove that tenacity and resilience are the keys to unlocking remarkable achievements. Their experiences serve as tangible examples of how perseverance can turn setbacks into stepping stones toward greatness.

Chapter Three
Reinvention and Innovation

*W*hen Steve Jobs returned to Apple in 1997, the company teetered on the brink of collapse. He undertook a remarkable reinvention of Apple's product line, introducing groundbreaking innovations such as the iMac, iPod, and iPhone. These innovations transformed Apple into a pioneer in technology, leaving an indelible mark on the industry.

Embracing Change and Adaptability

As an entrepreneur, one of the most important skills I have learned on my journey to success is the art of embracing change and adaptability. The business world is constantly evolving, and in order to thrive, it is crucial to stay nimble and be able to adjust our strategies accordingly. In this subchapter, we will discuss the importance of embracing change, provide strategies for identifying and seizing opportunities, and explore ways to adapt our business strategies to evolving market trends.

Change is inevitable, and those who resist it often find themselves left behind. In order to stay ahead of the game, it is essential to embrace change and be open to new ideas and perspectives. I vividly remember a time in my entrepreneurial journey when I was hesitant to embrace change. My business was struggling, and I was clinging onto the same old strategies that had worked in the past. However, it soon became clear that the market had shifted, and if I wanted to survive, I had to adapt.

This realization led me to embark on a journey of personal growth and self-discovery. I consumed books, attended workshops, and sought the advice of mentors who had successfully navigated through periods of change. Through this process, I began to understand that change is not something to be feared, but rather an opportunity for growth and innovation. I learned to let go of my ego and be open to new possibilities, and it was during this time that I experienced a profound transformation that would ultimately lead me to success.

In order to effectively embrace change, it is important to stay informed and be aware of the evolving market trends. This requires constant research and staying up to date with industry news and developments. I have found that subscribing to relevant industry publications, attending conferences, and engaging in networking events have been valuable in keeping me informed and connected to the pulse of the market.

Identifying opportunities in the midst of change is another crucial aspect of embracing change and adaptability. The ability to spot trends early on and take advantage of emerging opportunities can give entrepreneurs a competitive edge. This requires a keen sense of observation and the ability to connect seemingly unrelated dots. One strategy that has worked for me is to constantly ask myself, "What problem can I solve?" By seeking to identify problems and finding innovative solutions, I have been able to spot opportunities that others may have overlooked.

Once an opportunity is identified, it is important to act swiftly and decisively. In a rapidly changing market, timing is everything. I learned the hard way that hesitating or delaying can result in missed opportunities. To stay nimble, I have adopted a mindset of experimentation and fast iteration. By testing new ideas and measuring their impact quickly, I am able to adapt and adjust my strategies accordingly. This agile approach has allowed me to stay ahead of the curve and turn challenges into opportunities.

In addition to identifying and seizing opportunities, adapting our business strategies to evolving market trends is essential for long-term success. This requires a willingness to let go of the familiar and embrace new ways of doing things. It may involve reevaluating our business model, revising our marketing strategies, or even making tough decisions such as letting go of non-performing employees or reevaluating partnerships.

When adapting our business strategies, it is important to involve our team and communicate effectively. Change can be unsettling for employees, and it is crucial to make them feel included in the decision-making process. By fostering a culture of open communication and collaboration, we can ensure that everyone is aligned and working together towards a shared vision. In my experience, involving employees in the process of change not only increases buy-in and commitment but also leads to innovative ideas and solutions that may have otherwise been overlooked.

Lastly, it is important to remain resilient in the face of adversity. Change can be challenging, and there will inevitably be setbacks and roadblocks along the way. However, it is during these times that we have the opportunity to grow and learn the most. By maintaining a positive mindset, seeking support from mentors and like-minded entrepreneurs, and staying focused on our long-term goals, we can navigate through turbulent times and come out stronger on the other side.

Embracing change and adaptability is not just a skill; it is a mindset and way of life. It requires constant learning, curiosity, and a willingness to step outside our comfort zones. The business landscape will continue to evolve, and those who can adapt and embrace change will be the ones who not only survive but thrive. By staying nimble, seizing opportunities, and adjusting our strategies accordingly, we can write our own path to success and achieve the entrepreneurial redemption we seek.

Harnessing the Power of Innovation

Before delving into the depths of innovation and its significance, let me recount a personal anecdote that highlights the crucial nature of innovation in the entrepreneurial journey. It was during the darkest days of my business when I found myself teetering on the edge of bankruptcy. My once-thriving company was now struggling to stay afloat in a sea of competitors. It was at this pivotal moment that I realized the dire need for a fresh perspective, a radical departure from the status quo. Our once-thriving healthcare insurance solution was grappling with increased competition and outdated features that hindered efficiency. I needed innovation to lift me out of the depths of despair and into the path of redemption.

At this critical juncture, we knew that innovation was our only lifeline. We embarked on a journey to revolutionize our platform. The key innovation was the introduction of 'HealthGuard AI,' an unprecedented and futuristic feature powered by artificial intelligence. HealthGuard AI could predict health risks for policyholders, helping them take proactive measures to maintain well-being. It was a game-changer, setting us apart in the industry.

We didn't stop there. To promote this innovation, we launched an aggressive digital marketing campaign. We utilized personalized email campaigns, social media advertising, and even virtual reality presentations to demonstrate the capabilities of HealthGuard AI. This digital marketing strategy positioned us as pioneers and attracted a surge of interest from policyholders and healthcare providers.

Our innovative approach and futuristic features not only saved our business from bankruptcy but propelled us to the forefront of the healthcare insurance industry. It served as a remarkable example of how innovation, coupled with an aggressive digital marketing strategy, can transform adversity into opportunity, even in the darkest moments of an entrepreneurial journey.

I began by understanding the different forms of innovation and the unique benefits they offer. Product innovation, for instance, involves the development of new and improved products or services that cater to the ever-changing needs and desires of consumers. It could be as simple as adding new features to an existing product or as complex as reinventing an entire industry with a groundbreaking invention. By actively seeking product innovation, businesses can stay ahead of the curve, outshine their competitors, and capture the attention and loyalty of their target market.

Process innovation, on the other hand, focuses on finding more efficient and effective ways of doing things. It involves streamlining operational processes, reducing costs, improving quality control, and enhancing overall organizational efficiency. In an increasingly competitive market, process innovation can be the difference between surviving and thriving. By constantly seeking ways to optimize and improve internal systems, businesses can transform their operations from stagnant to dynamic, enabling them to deliver better products and services to their customers at lower costs and higher availability.

Both product innovation and process innovation are vital aspects of long-term business success. They go hand in hand, driving growth, and enabling sustainable competitive advantage. However, merely recognizing the importance of innovation is not enough. Entrepreneurs must actively cultivate a culture that celebrates and nurtures innovation.

This brings me to the crux of this subchapter: providing practical tips for fostering a culture of innovation within an organization.

First and foremost, fostering a culture of innovation begins with leadership. As an entrepreneur, I have come to realize that my role extends far beyond visionary ideas and strategic decisions. I must serve as a champion and advocate for innovation, leading by example and motivating my team to think creatively and embrace novelty. By openly valuing and supporting innovative ideas, entrepreneurs can create an environment where employees feel empowered to take risks and explore new horizons.

Another key aspect of fostering a culture of innovation is promoting collaboration and cross-pollination of ideas. Innovations rarely arise in isolation; they thrive when different perspectives come together in an environment that encourages open dialogue and knowledge-sharing. By facilitating diverse team compositions, encouraging brainstorming sessions, and providing avenues for cross-functional collaboration, entrepreneurs can foster a rich and fertile ground for innovative thinking.

Furthermore, entrepreneurs must encourage experimentation and embrace failure as an inherent part of the innovation process. The fear of failure often stifles creativity and inhibits the pursuit of bold ideas. In an innovative culture, mistakes are not perceived as setbacks, but rather as stepping stones on the path to success. By fostering an environment where calculated risks are encouraged, entrepreneurs can unlock the hidden potential of their employees and pave the way for groundbreaking discoveries.

Additionally, entrepreneurs should prioritize continuous learning and development. Innovation does not happen in a vacuum; it requires a mindset that is constantly seeking new knowledge and staying updated with the latest advancements in their respective industries. By investing in employee training programs, providing resources for self-learning, and encouraging professional development, entrepreneurs can cultivate a workforce that is equipped with the skills and knowledge necessary to drive innovation forward.

Lastly, recognition and rewards play a crucial role in fostering a culture of innovation. Celebrating and acknowledging the efforts and successes of employees who contribute to innovative ideas not only boosts morale but also reinforces the importance of innovation within the organization. By implementing reward programs, fostering a sense of ownership, and providing opportunities for advancement, entrepreneurs can foster a culture where innovation becomes ingrained in the fabric of the organization.

In conclusion, innovation is the backbone of business success in today's fast-paced entrepreneurial landscape. Whether it is product innovation or process innovation, entrepreneurs must recognize the transformative power innovation holds and actively cultivate a culture that nurtures and celebrates novelty. By leading by example, promoting collaboration, embracing failure, prioritizing continuous learning, and recognizing and rewarding innovative efforts, entrepreneurs can harness the power of innovation and pave the way for their redemption from the depths of failure to the heights of success.

Disruptive Technologies and Trends

In today's rapidly changing world, staying ahead of the curve is vital for any entrepreneur. The landscape of business is constantly evolving, and entrepreneurs need to adapt to these changes to survive and thrive. This subchapter delves into the realm of disruptive technologies and emerging trends, exploring their impact on the entrepreneurial ecosystem and how they can be utilized to unlock new possibilities.

Disruptive technologies refer to innovations that completely transform an industry or market by creating new business models and challenging existing norms. These technologies often emerge unexpectedly and catch established players off guard. However, for entrepreneurs, they present an opportunity to disrupt the status quo and pave the way for a new era of innovation.

One example of a disruptive technology is artificial intelligence (AI). AI has the potential to revolutionize multiple industries, from healthcare and finance to transportation and logistics. Entrepreneurs who are quick to embrace AI can gain a significant competitive advantage by leveraging its capabilities to automate processes, optimize decision-making, and improve overall efficiency. By integrating AI into their products or services, entrepreneurs can deliver a superior customer experience and differentiate themselves from their competitors.

The emergence of the Internet of Things (IoT) is another disruptive trend that entrepreneurs should keep an eye on. The IoT refers to the network of physical objects embedded with sensors, software, and connectivity that enables them to collect and exchange data. This technology has the potential to transform industries such as manufacturing, agriculture, and healthcare.

Entrepreneurs can leverage the data generated by IoT devices to gain insights into customer behaviors, optimize operations, and create personalized experiences. By capitalizing on the power of the IoT, entrepreneurs can create innovative solutions that meet the evolving needs of their target market.

Blockchain technology is yet another disruptive force that entrepreneurs should not overlook. Initially popularized by the rise of cryptocurrencies like Bitcoin, blockchain has the potential to revolutionize various industries beyond finance. Its decentralized and transparent nature provides entrepreneurs with an opportunity to create secure and efficient solutions for tasks such as supply chain management, identity verification, and intellectual property protection. Blockchain's ability to enhance trust, reduce costs, and streamline processes makes it an invaluable tool for entrepreneurs looking to disrupt traditional industries.

Let us also explore other emerging trends such as sustainable entrepreneurship and the sharing economy. Sustainable entrepreneurship focuses on creating businesses that are not only financially viable but also environmentally and socially responsible. Entrepreneurs who embrace sustainability can attract a growing group of conscious consumers who prioritize ethical practices and environmental stewardship. This trend opens doors for entrepreneurs to develop innovative solutions that address pressing global challenges, such as climate change and resource scarcity.

The sharing economy, on the other hand, is a collaborative economic model that allows individuals and businesses to share resources, such as goods, services, and even physical space. Platforms like Uber and Airbnb have disrupted traditional industries, and entrepreneurs can take advantage of this trend by creating similar platforms that connect underutilized resources with those in need. By embracing the sharing economy, entrepreneurs can tap into new markets, reduce costs, and drive innovation.

To successfully leverage these disruptive technologies and emerging trends, entrepreneurs must adopt a forward-thinking mindset and continuously adapt to the changing landscape. They need to stay up to date with the latest advancements, identify gaps in the market, and seize opportunities to innovate. Additionally, collaboration and strategic partnerships with technology companies or other entrepreneurs can provide access to expertise and resources that are critical for success in disruptive environments.

Continuous Learning and Personal Growth

The journey begins in the early 19th century, amidst the backdrop of the Industrial Revolution. It was a time of tremendous growth and transformation, as new technologies, such as the steam engine, revolutionized manufacturing processes. Entrepreneurs of this era were pioneers, constantly adapting to the changing economic landscape and seeking out opportunities to expand and innovate.

One influential figure during this period was Benjamin Franklin, an American polymath and one of the founding fathers of the United States. Franklin believed deeply in the power of learning and personal growth, famously stating, "An investment in knowledge pays the best interest." His entrepreneurial endeavors ranged from publishing to inventing, and he continuously sought to improve his skills and knowledge through self-guided study and experimentation.

As the 19th century progressed, the concept of entrepreneurship continued to evolve. The rise of capitalism and the expansion of global trade created new opportunities for ambitious individuals to create their own businesses. Many entrepreneurs of this era, such as Andrew Carnegie and John D. Rockefeller, amassed vast fortunes through their innovative business practices and relentless pursuit of knowledge.

During the early 20th century, the world witnessed the emergence of major industries such as oil, automobiles, and telecommunications. Entrepreneurs like Henry Ford and Thomas Edison became household names, not only for their achievements in these industries but also for their dedication to continuous learning. Ford, for instance, famously said, "Anyone who stops learning is old, whether at 20 or 80. Anyone who keeps learning stays young."

With the dawn of the digital age in the late 20th century, entrepreneurship took on a new dimension. The rapid advancement of technology brought about unprecedented opportunities for innovation and disruption. Entrepreneurs such as Steve Jobs and Mark Zuckerberg revolutionized the way we communicate and interact with the world, forever changing the landscape of business.

In today's fast-paced, interconnected world, the need for continuous learning and personal growth has never been more critical. The global marketplace is constantly evolving, driven by advancements in technology, shifting consumer preferences, and changing regulatory landscapes. Entrepreneurs must adapt to these changes to remain competitive and relevant.

One effective strategy for achieving continuous learning and personal growth is through attending workshops and conferences. These events provide entrepreneurs with the opportunity to learn from industry experts, gain insights into emerging trends, and network with like-minded individuals. The knowledge and connections gained from these experiences can be invaluable in navigating the ever-changing business landscape.

Seeking mentorship is another powerful learning strategy for entrepreneurs. Mentors, who are experienced and successful individuals in their respective fields, can provide guidance, advice, and valuable insights based on their own experiences. By working closely with a mentor, entrepreneurs can accelerate their learning curve, avoid common pitfalls, and gain access to a wealth of knowledge and resources.

Keeping abreast of industry developments is also essential for entrepreneurs. In today's digital age, information is readily available at our fingertips. Entrepreneurs must make a conscious effort to stay informed about the latest trends, technologies, and market dynamics affecting their industries. This can be done through reading industry publications, following influential thought leaders on social media, and engaging in online communities and forums.

However, continuous learning and personal growth go beyond simply acquiring knowledge. It also involves developing key skills and qualities that are necessary for success in entrepreneurship. These may include critical thinking, problem-solving, creativity, adaptability, and resilience. By honing these skills, entrepreneurs can better navigate the challenges and uncertainties that come with running a business.

Furthermore, personal growth is intrinsically linked to professional growth. As entrepreneurs strive to grow their businesses and achieve their goals, they must also invest in their personal development. This may involve developing emotional intelligence, improving communication and leadership skills, or enhancing self-awareness. By cultivating these qualities, entrepreneurs can effectively manage themselves and their teams, fostering a positive and productive work environment.

Reinventing the Entrepreneurial Identity

As entrepreneurs, our journey is never a linear one. It is a constant ebb and flow of successes and failures, highs and lows. And in these moments of uncertainty and self-doubt, it is essential to take a step back and engage in self-reflection.

Self-reflection is not merely a fleeting moment of introspection; it is a deliberate process of diving deep into one's thoughts, emotions, and experiences. It requires us to question our beliefs, values, and assumptions, and to confront our fears and insecurities head-on.

In order to reinvent our entrepreneurial identity, we must first understand who we are and what drives us. We must ask ourselves tough questions:

Why do we do what we do? What are our ultimate goals? What are our strengths and weaknesses?

For me, self-reflection took the form of journaling. Every morning, I would carve out a few moments to jot down my thoughts and feelings. It was during these quiet moments of introspection that I began to uncover the underlying patterns and motivations that shaped my entrepreneurial journey.

I also found solace in seeking the perspectives of others. I surrounded myself with a trusted group of mentors and advisors who could provide valuable insight and guidance. Their external perspectives helped me gain a clearer understanding of my own strengths and weaknesses, ultimately enabling me to redefine my entrepreneurial identity. Once we have gained a better understanding of ourselves, it is time to embark on a journey of self-improvement. We cannot reinvent our entrepreneurial identity without continuously evolving and growing as individuals.

Self-improvement encompasses a wide range of pursuits, from honing our skills and acquiring new knowledge to challenging our comfort zones and embracing change. It requires a commitment to lifelong learning and a willingness to adapt to the ever-changing landscape of entrepreneurship.

One aspect of self-improvement that I delved into was personal development. I sought out books, podcasts, and courses that focused on topics such as leadership, emotional intelligence, and mindset. These resources not only expanded my knowledge but also inspired me to become a better version of myself.

Another area of self-improvement that was crucial in reinventing my entrepreneurial identity was skill development. I identified the skills that were lacking or needed improvement and actively sought out opportunities to develop them. Whether it was attending workshops, joining networking events, or collaborating with other professionals, I made a conscious effort to continuously refine my skills.

Self-improvement also involves taking risks and embracing failure. It is through failure that we learn the most valuable lessons and uncover new opportunities for growth. By reframing failure as a learning experience rather than a setback, we can unlock our true potential and reinvent our entrepreneurial identity.

Embracing New Roles and Responsibilities

As we evolve in our entrepreneurial journey, our roles and responsibilities inevitably change. We must be willing to let go of our old identity and embrace the new challenges and opportunities that come our way.

One key aspect of embracing new roles and responsibilities is learning to delegate. As entrepreneurs, we often wear multiple hats and try to do everything ourselves. However, as our businesses grow, it becomes crucial to trust and empower others to take on certain tasks. Delegating not only relieves us of unnecessary burdens but also allows us to focus on our core strengths and strategic initiatives.

Another important aspect of embracing new roles and responsibilities is adapting to changing market trends and customer needs. The entrepreneurial landscape is dynamic, and what worked in the past may not work in the future. We must be open to pivoting our business models, exploring new markets, and embracing innovation. This requires a willingness to step out of our comfort zones and challenge the status quo.

Furthermore, embracing new roles and responsibilities means becoming a leader. As entrepreneurs, we are not only responsible for our own success but also for the success of our teams. This requires developing strong leadership skills, fostering a culture of collaboration and growth, and empowering others to achieve their full potential.

Chapter Four
Lessons Learned

Richard Branson's entrepreneurial journey included an attempt to diversify into Virgin Cola. However, this venture proved to be a costly mistake. Branson learned valuable lessons about the importance of focusing on core businesses, redirecting his attention and resources toward successful ventures like Virgin Records and Virgin Atlantic.

Lessons and Insights

First and foremost, one of the most important lessons I learned was the significance of perseverance. The road to success is rarely smooth and straightforward. It is riddled with obstacles, setbacks, and numerous moments of doubt. However, it is during these challenging times that true entrepreneurs are separated from the rest. They possess an unwavering determination, a refusal to give up, and the ability to adapt and overcome any adversity that comes their way.

Another important lesson I gained from my entrepreneurial journey was the value of calculated risks. In the world of business, taking risks is an inherent part of the process. However, it is crucial to separate reckless gambles from calculated risks that can potentially yield significant rewards. Throughout my journey, I have learned to carefully evaluate every opportunity that presents itself, weighing the potential benefits against the risks involved.

There were moments when I had to make difficult decisions that seemed risky at the time. I took calculated risks by investing in new ventures and expanding my business into untapped markets. These decisions were not made lightly, but they ultimately propelled me towards success. It was through these experiences that I developed a keen intuition for recognizing opportunities and making bold moves when necessary.

Additionally, my entrepreneurial journey has taught me the importance of effective communication and the power of building strong relationships. Success rarely comes in isolation; it is often the result of collaborative efforts and the ability to connect with others. I have realized that fostering genuine and meaningful relationships with my employees, partners, and clients has been instrumental in my personal and professional growth.

I recall a pivotal moment when a major client threatened to terminate our contract due to a misunderstanding. Instead of becoming defensive or confrontational, I took the time to sit down with the client and actively listen to their concerns. Through open and honest communication, I was able to address the issues at hand and find a mutually beneficial solution. This experience taught me that effective communication is not just about articulating one's thoughts but also about actively listening to others and finding common ground.

Lastly, my entrepreneurial journey has taught me the importance of maintaining a healthy work-life balance. In the pursuit of success, it is easy to become consumed by work, neglecting other important aspects of life such as relationships, hobbies, and personal well-being. However, I have come to realize that true success lies not only in professional achievements but also in leading a fulfilling and balanced life.

Throughout my journey, I have made a conscious effort to prioritize self-care and invest time and energy into my personal life. This has allowed me to recharge, gain perspective, and bring a renewed sense of passion and creativity to my work. By establishing boundaries and setting aside time for relaxation and rejuvenation, I have been able to achieve both personal and professional fulfillment.

Broader Principles

One of the key principles I've discovered is the importance of perseverance. In the face of adversity and failure, it can be easy to give up and throw in the towel. However, by persevering through the tough times and staying committed to my goals, I was able to turn my business around and achieve the success I dreamed of. This principle applies not only to entrepreneurship but also to personal growth. It teaches us to keep pushing forward, even when the odds are stacked against us, and to never stop striving for our dreams.

Another principle that has been instrumental in my journey is the power of resilience. Entrepreneurship is full of ups and downs, and setbacks are inevitable. However, it is how we respond to these setbacks that truly define us. Resilience is about bouncing back from failure and using it as a learning opportunity. It is about finding the strength to get back up, dust ourselves off, and keep moving forward. This principle has not only helped me overcome obstacles in my business but has also taught me to embrace challenges and view them as opportunities for growth.

Additionally, I have learned the importance of adaptability in both entrepreneurship and personal growth. The business landscape is constantly evolving, and being able to adapt to change is crucial for success. In my own journey, I had to pivot my business strategy multiple times to stay relevant and meet the ever-changing demands of the market. Similarly, personal growth requires us to be adaptable and open to new experiences and perspectives. By embracing change and being willing to step outside of our comfort zones, we can continue to learn, grow, and evolve.

A principle that cannot be overlooked is the power of passion. Entrepreneurship is not easy, and without passion, it can be challenging to persevere through the inevitable difficulties. Passion fuels our drive and determination, giving us the motivation to push through obstacles and make our dreams a reality. It is also a catalyst for personal growth, as being passionate about something ignites a fire within us and drives us to become the best version of ourselves.

Another principle that I have come to appreciate is the value of strategic thinking. As an entrepreneur, it is important to have a clear vision and a well-thought-out plan. Strategic thinking involves analyzing different options, assessing risks, and making informed decisions. This principle has guided my business decisions, allowing me to make calculated moves and avoid unnecessary risks. It has also taught me to think critically and strategically in all areas of my life, enabling me to approach challenges and opportunities with a logical and well-rounded perspective.

Lastly, I have learned the importance of surrounding myself with a strong support system. Entrepreneurship can be a lonely and overwhelming journey, and having the support and guidance of others can make all the difference. Whether it's mentors, advisors, or a network of like-minded individuals, having a support system provides not only valuable insights but also a sense of community and encouragement. Personal growth is also enhanced by the support of others who believe in us and push us to become the best version of ourselves.

Chapter Five
Leadership and Team Building

*B*ill Gates, the co-founder of Microsoft, demonstrated visionary leadership by fostering a collaborative work environment. He built a cohesive team that operated as a united force, instilling a culture of innovation within the company. This approach allowed Microsoft to reach global prominence within the tech industry.

The Qualities of Effective Leaders

One of the key qualities of effective leaders is their ability to adapt their leadership style to different situations and individuals. Leadership is not a one-size-fits-all approach. Different circumstances require different approaches, and great leaders understand this intuitively. They can be autocratic when the situation demands quick and decisive action, but they can also be democratic when seeking to involve their team members in decision-making processes. By adapting their leadership style, effective leaders are able to create a sense of trust and collaboration among their team members.

Another crucial quality of effective leaders is their strong communication skills. A leader who can communicate effectively can articulate their vision, goals, and expectations clearly to their team members. They are also adept at listening and understanding the needs, concerns, and ideas of their team. This two-way communication fosters an environment of open dialogue and trust, where team members feel valued and motivated to contribute their best work.

Moreover, effective leaders possess the ability to inspire and motivate others. They have a clear sense of purpose and are able to communicate that purpose in a way that inspires their team members. They lead by example, demonstrating the values and behaviors they expect from their team. By doing so, they create a sense of trust and loyalty among their team members, who are inspired to go above and beyond in their work. Effective leaders also understand the importance of recognizing and celebrating the achievements of their team members. They create a culture of appreciation and motivation, leading to increased productivity and satisfaction within the team.

In addition to these qualities, effective leaders also exhibit a high degree of emotional intelligence. They have a deep understanding of their own emotions and the ability to manage them effectively, which allows them to stay calm and composed under pressure. They also empathize with the emotions of their team members and are able to respond in a supportive and empathetic manner. This emotional intelligence enables effective leaders to build strong relationships with their team members and create a positive and inclusive work environment.

Furthermore, effective leaders are continuously learning and growing. They understand that leadership is a journey, not a destination, and are committed to self-improvement. They seek feedback and actively work on their weaknesses, constantly striving to become better leaders.

Effective leaders also encourage a culture of learning within their team, fostering an environment where everyone feels encouraged to develop their skills and knowledge.

In summary, the qualities and characteristics of effective leaders are multifaceted and complex. They require a combination of adaptability, communication skills, inspiration, emotional intelligence, and a commitment to continual learning and growth. As an entrepreneur, I strive to embody these qualities and constantly work on developing and refining them. By doing so, I believe I can create a positive and impactful leadership style that inspires and empowers my team members to reach their full potential. Through the journey of becoming an effective leader, I have experienced my own redemption, transforming from a struggling entrepreneur to a successful businessperson.

Building and Managing High-Performing Teams

As an entrepreneur, I learned early on that a successful business is only as strong as the team driving it forward. Building and managing high-performing teams became a top priority for me as I witnessed the transformational effects it had on my own ventures. I will share with you here the strategies I've discovered for recruiting top talent, fostering teamwork, and creating a culture of trust and accountability within your organization.

Recruiting Top Talent: The first step in building a high-performing team is attracting top talent to join your ranks. Finding individuals with the right skill-set, mindset, and cultural fit is essential. This is not a task to be taken lightly, as the success of your team hinges on the individuals you bring on board. To begin, I learned the importance of clearly defining what qualities and skills are needed for each role in my organization. This allowed me to craft targeted job descriptions and specifications that would attract the right candidates. But it wasn't enough to simply attract potential hires; I had to convince them that my organization was their best career move.

To do this, I fine-tuned my recruitment process to showcase the unique opportunities and growth potential that my company offered. I highlighted the impact they could make, the challenges they would face, and the support they would receive. By presenting a compelling vision and demonstrating a commitment to their professional development, I found that top talent was more likely to choose my organization over others.

Fostering Teamwork: Once you have assembled a team of exceptional individuals, the next challenge is fostering an environment where they can work collaboratively and seamlessly together. I understood that teamwork is not just about individuals working side by side, but about synergy and shared goals.

To achieve this, I focused on two key aspects: communication and trust.

Effective communication is critical in any team setting, and I quickly implemented strategies to ensure that information flowed freely and efficiently among team members. This included regular team meetings, one-on-one check-ins, and the use of collaboration tools to facilitate seamless communication.

Creating a culture of trust was equally important. I encouraged open and honest communication, creating a safe space for team members to voice their opinions, concerns, and ideas without fear of judgment or retribution. I also led by example, demonstrating trust in my team and their abilities. This fostered an environment where trust became the foundation of our team dynamics.

Additionally, I recognized the value of celebrating both individual and team achievements. Recognizing and rewarding exceptional performance not only boosts morale but also reinforces the sense of camaraderie and teamwork among team members. I implemented regular feedback sessions, where both individual and collective accomplishments were acknowledged and appreciated.

Creating a Culture of Trust and Accountability: To truly maximize the potential of a high-performing team, it is essential to create a culture of trust and accountability. Trust enables team members to collaborate effectively, while accountability ensures that everyone takes ownership of their responsibilities.

In order to establish trust within my team, I made an effort to be transparent and honest in my communications. I shared information, both good and bad, ensuring that everyone had the necessary insights to make informed decisions. I also encouraged open dialogue and active listening, valuing the opinions and perspectives of each team member.

Accountability was fostered through clear goal-setting and regular performance evaluations. I made sure that every team member had a clear understanding of their roles and responsibilities, and I held them accountable for meeting these expectations. This was done through a combination of regular check-ins, performance metrics, and feedback sessions. By setting high standards and providing support, I encouraged my team to take ownership of their work and strive for excellence.

Furthermore, I emphasized the importance of continuous learning and improvement within our team culture. I encouraged team members to pursue professional development opportunities, invest in their skill sets, and share knowledge within the team. By fostering a culture of continuous growth, our team was able to stay ahead of the curve and adapt to ever-changing market dynamics.

Remember, success is a journey best traveled together, with a team unified in purpose and driven by shared goals.

The Art of Delegation

To fully grasp the significance of delegation, let's take a step back and explore its historical context. Throughout the centuries, great leaders have understood the value of shared responsibilities. The ancient Chinese military strategist, Sun Tzu, famously remarked, "He who tries to do everything himself will surely become exhausted." These words hold true even in our modern, fast-paced business world.

One of the earliest examples of effective delegation can be traced back to Julius Caesar, the renowned Roman military general. Caesar understood that to conquer vast territories, he needed to rely on his most trusted lieutenants. He strategically delegated tasks to his subordinates, allowing him to focus on broader objectives. This not only increased his own efficiency but also empowered his team members to take ownership of their roles.

Fast forward to the present day, and the art of delegation remains as relevant as ever. In fact, in today's complex business environment, delegation has become a prerequisite for sustainable growth. As entrepreneurs, we often find ourselves carrying the weight of multiple tasks and responsibilities. We juggle marketing strategies, financial planning, team management, and more – all while trying to steer our businesses towards success.

But the truth is, we can't do it all on our own. Trying to take on everything not only leads to exhaustion but also hinders growth and limits our ability to innovate. Delegation, therefore, becomes essential in order to maximize productivity and efficiency.

So, how do we effectively delegate tasks and empower our team members? Here are some practical tips to get you started:

1. ***Clearly define roles and responsibilities:*** Before delegating any task, it is crucial to define roles and responsibilities. This ensures that everyone understands their areas of expertise and can make informed decisions. By clarifying expectations, you are setting your team members up for success and promoting a sense of ownership in their work.

2. ***Identify strengths and weaknesses:*** Take the time to identify the strengths and weaknesses of each team member. This will allow you to delegate tasks that align with their skill set, increasing the likelihood of successful outcomes. Understanding your team's capabilities will also help you identify areas where additional training or resources may be required.

3. ***Establish clear communication channels:*** Effective delegation requires open and transparent communication channels. Regularly check in with your team members to offer guidance and support. Encourage them to share progress updates and any challenges they may be facing. This open dialogue fosters a culture of trust and ensures that everyone is on the same page.

4. ***Provide adequate resources:*** When delegating tasks, it is essential to provide your team members with the resources they need to succeed. Whether it's access to tools, training, or additional staff, ensure that your team has everything necessary to complete the delegated tasks efficiently. Investing in your team's success will yield long-term benefits for your business.

5. ***Balance control with trust:*** Delegating tasks can sometimes be challenging for entrepreneurs who are used to maintaining tight control over every aspect of their business. However, it is important to find a balance between control and trust. Give your team members autonomy to make decisions and take ownership of their work, while still providing guidance and mentorship when needed.

6. ***Evaluate and celebrate success:*** Once a task has been delegated and completed, take the time to evaluate the outcome. Recognize and celebrate the successes achieved by your team members. This not only boosts morale but also reinforces the importance of delegation and encourages a culture of continuous improvement.

By embracing the art of delegation, we unlock the potential for exponential growth in our business. We give ourselves the freedom to focus on strategic vision and innovation while empowering our team members to grow and excel. Delegation is an art that requires practice and refinement, but the rewards are immeasurable.

I invite you to reflect on your own style of leadership and identify areas where delegation can be integrated into your business. Remember, true success lies in the ability to trust in your team members, harness their expertise, and together, create a sustainable and prosperous future.

Conflict Resolution and Collaboration

Conflict resolution and fostering collaboration are essential elements for the success of any team. In this subchapter, we delve into the common challenges faced in resolving conflicts and building a harmonious work environment. We will explore strategies for effectively managing conflicts, promoting open communication, and nurturing teamwork to ensure a positive and productive collaboration within a team.

Conflicts are inevitable in any team. Diverse personalities, opinions, and objectives often lead to disagreements and tensions. However, conflicts, if not handled properly, can hinder progress and affect team dynamics. It is crucial to acknowledge and address conflicts, fostering an environment that promotes open communication and cooperation. By doing so, conflicts can be transformed into opportunities for growth and innovation.

The Challenges of Conflict Resolution

Resolving conflicts within a team can be a complex and delicate process. Often, individuals involved are emotionally invested in their own perspectives and reluctant to compromise or understand opposing viewpoints. The following are some common challenges one might encounter during conflict resolution:

a. ***Ego and Personal Bias:*** An egocentric mindset and the presence of personal biases can hinder the ability to objectively analyze conflicts. Often, individuals are more focused on being right rather than finding a mutually beneficial solution.
b. ***Lack of Effective Communication:*** Poor communication or misinterpretation of messages can escalate conflicts. When individuals fail to express their thoughts and emotions clearly, misunderstandings arise, and tensions increase.
c. ***Power Struggles:*** Conflicts can arise when there is a disparity in power dynamics within a team. If individuals feel their authority or value is undermined, they may react defensively or aggressively, exacerbating conflicts.

Strategies for Conflict Resolution

1. ***Promoting Open Communication:***
   One of the key strategies for effective conflict resolution is promoting open communication within the team. Encouraging individuals to express their thoughts, concerns, and frustrations openly can help diffuse tensions and pave the way for greater understanding. Here are some techniques to foster open communication:

   - *Active Listening:* Actively listen to the perspectives of all individuals involved, allowing them to feel heard and understood. This demonstrates respect and creates an enabling environment for collaboration.

   - *Encouraging Dialogue:* Create opportunities for open dialogue where team members can express their viewpoints without fear of judgment or retribution. This encourages collaboration and helps identify common ground among conflicting ideas.

   - *Constructive Feedback:* Provide constructive feedback to individuals involved in conflicts, emphasizing the importance of constructive criticism rather than personal attacks. This allows for growth and improvement, leading to better collaboration.

2. ***Encouraging Empathy:***
   Empathy plays a crucial role in conflict resolution. When individuals are able to understand and relate to the emotions and perspectives of others, conflicts can be approached with compassion and the desire for a mutually beneficial solution. Here are some strategies to encourage empathy:

- ***Perspective-Taking:*** Encourage team members to put themselves in each other's shoes to understand the underlying motivations and emotions behind conflicting viewpoints. This helps cultivate empathy and promotes a deeper understanding of each other's perspectives.

- ***Emotional Intelligence Development:*** Foster emotional intelligence within the team, enabling individuals to recognize and manage their own emotions as well as empathize with others. Emotional intelligence helps individuals navigate conflicts more effectively and build stronger relationships.

3. *Facilitating Collaborative Problem-Solving:*

Collaborative problem-solving is a powerful technique for conflict resolution. By involving all team members and encouraging them to contribute ideas and solutions, conflicts can be addressed creatively and collaboratively. Here are some techniques to facilitate collaborative problem-solving:

- ***Brainstorming Sessions:*** Conduct brainstorming sessions where all team members are encouraged to contribute ideas to resolve conflicts. This promotes a sense of ownership and shared responsibility for finding solutions.

- ***Mediation and Facilitation:*** Appoint a neutral third party to mediate in conflicts, ensuring fairness and facilitating communication between conflicting parties. Mediation helps create a safe space for open dialogue and supports reaching a compromise.

- ***Team-Building Activities:*** Engage in team-building activities that foster trust and collaboration among team members. Activities such as problem-solving games or retreats help build stronger relationships and enable individuals to work together more effectively.

Building a Harmonious Work Environment

Creating a harmonious work environment is crucial for fostering collaboration and conflict resolution. When team members feel supported, valued, and respected, conflicts are less likely to escalate and hinder productivity.

Here are some strategies to build a harmonious work environment:

- *Clear Communication of Expectations:* Clearly communicate team goals, roles, and responsibilities to ensure all members are on the same page. This reduces ambiguity and promotes a sense of direction and purpose.

- *Organizational Culture:* Foster an organizational culture that encourages open communication, diversity, and inclusion. By creating an environment that values different perspectives and supports collaboration, conflicts can be resolved more effectively.

- *Conflict Resolution Training:* Provide conflict resolution training to team members, equipping them with the necessary skills to identify and address conflicts proactively. This empowers individuals to resolve conflicts independently and creates a culture of continuous improvement. Conflict resolution and collaboration are vital aspects of teamwork and organizational success. By understanding and addressing the challenges involved in conflict resolution, fostering open communication, and promoting a harmonious work environment, teams can overcome conflicts and work together more effectively. Remember, conflicts are opportunities for growth and innovation; embracing them with empathy and collaboration can lead to the redemption of any entrepreneur.

Cultivating a Positive Work Culture

A positive work culture is not just a fluff term tossed around in management books and seminars. It is a fundamental component that sets the stage for an organization's success or failure. As an entrepreneur who has experienced both sides of the spectrum, I can confidently say that creating a positive work culture was the turning point in my journey The Resilient Entrepreneur.

To understand the significance of cultivating a positive work culture, we must first examine its roots. Throughout history, the workplace has often been portrayed as a relentless battle zone, where employees were treated as mere cogs in a giant machinery. However, over time, societal and cultural shifts have brought about a gradual transformation in how we perceive work. Gone are the days when employees were simply expected to show up, punch the clock, and carry out their tasks mindlessly.

Research has shown that a supportive and inclusive work culture has a profound impact on employee morale. When individuals feel valued and appreciated, their motivation and commitment soar. In my own journey as an entrepreneur, I vividly recall the transformation that occurred in my team once we prioritized creating a positive work environment. Suddenly, employees became more invested in their work, going above and beyond their prescribed duties. The collective energy in the office was palpable, and it translated into tangible results.

Productivity, perhaps the most coveted metric for any business, is directly linked to work culture. Countless studies have shown that employees who work in positive environments are more productive and engaged. This is not surprising when you consider how much time individuals spend in their workplaces. It is only logical that a healthy work environment nurtures productivity and fuels innovation.

As an entrepreneur who has experienced the negative consequences of an unhealthy work culture, I can attest to the detrimental effects it can have on business success. In the early days of my entrepreneurial journey, I focused solely on the bottom line and failed to recognize the immense impact of work culture on my company's growth. The result was stagnant productivity, high turnover rates, and a toxic atmosphere that permeated every corner of the office. It took a humbling reality check to open my eyes to the importance of cultivating a positive work culture.

Creating a positive work culture is not a one-time event, but an ongoing process that requires commitment and effort. It begins with leadership, as individuals at the helm must set the tone and lead by example. When leaders prioritize transparency, communication, and mutual respect, the foundations of a positive work culture are firmly established.

Inclusivity is a key aspect of cultivating a positive work culture. Companies that embrace diversity and inclusivity have been shown to outperform their competitors. When employees feel valued for their unique perspectives and are given opportunities to contribute, it fosters a sense of belonging and a shared purpose. This, in turn, leads to increased creativity and innovation, fueling the business's success.

Moreover, a positive work culture extends beyond the office walls. It infiltrates every interaction, every decision, and every aspect of an organization's operation. It becomes the guiding principle that shapes the company's values, policies, and practices. In my own company, I made a conscious effort to align our work culture with our core values. By doing so, we not only attracted top talent but also built a strong reputation that attracted clients and partners who shared our vision.

Creating a positive work culture is an investment that yields immeasurable returns. It not only attracts and retains top talent but also helps businesses thrive in an increasingly competitive landscape. As an entrepreneur who has witnessed the transformative power of a positive work culture, I urge my fellow entrepreneurs to prioritize this aspect of their business. The journey The Resilient Entrepreneur begins with a commitment to cultivating a positive work culture. It is the key that unlocks the door to success and redemption.

Chapter Six
Strategic Planning and Execution

Jeff Bezos, Amazon's founder, meticulously planned the company's growth and expansion. With strategic brilliance, he guided Amazon into e-commerce, cloud computing, and various ventures. This calculated approach transformed Amazon into a global e-commerce giant and a pioneer in diverse industries.

Setting SMART Goals

SMART is an acronym that stands for Specific, Measurable, Achievable, Relevant, and Time-bound. These five qualities are essential for setting effective goals that drive progress and ensure that each milestone takes the business closer to its ultimate vision.

Specific Goals:

Specific goals help entrepreneurs pinpoint exactly what they want to achieve. For instance, instead of setting a vague goal like "increase sales," a specific goal would be "increase sales by 20% within the next quarter." By clearly defining the desired outcome, entrepreneurs can focus their efforts on the specific actions required to attain that goal.

Measurable Goals:

Measurable goals allow entrepreneurs to track progress and determine whether they are on the right path. In our example of increasing sales by 20%, it becomes easier to measure success by monitoring monthly sales figures or analyzing customer feedback. Measurability brings clarity, enabling entrepreneurs to make data-driven decisions and adjust strategies accordingly.

Achievable Goals:

Achievable goals are realistic and attainable. It is important to set goals that challenge the business without being overly ambitious. For instance, aiming to increase sales by 200% within a month might not be realistic, as it may require significant changes in the business's infrastructure and resources. By setting achievable goals, entrepreneurs can maintain motivation and avoid setting themselves up for failure.

Relevant Goals:

Relevant goals are aligned with the overall vision and mission of the business. Every goal should contribute to the overarching objectives and reinforce the values and purpose of the company. For example, if a business's mission is to provide affordable and sustainable products, setting a goal to reduce waste by 30% would be relevant. Ensuring relevance fosters a sense of purpose and ensures that goals are aligned with the business's long-term trajectory.

Time-bound Goals:

Time-bound goals have a specific timeframe within which they should be accomplished. This aspect of SMART goal-setting urges entrepreneurs to establish a sense of urgency and prioritize tasks effectively. A goal without a defined timeline can easily be delayed or pushed aside, hindering progress and potentially derailing the business. By attaching deadlines to goals, entrepreneurs maintain momentum and hold themselves accountable.

While SMART goals provide a framework for effective goal-setting, entrepreneurs must also consider the broader context of their businesses. Goals should not be formulated in isolation; they must align with the overarching vision and mission of the company. This alignment ensures that every goal contributes to the bigger picture and keeps the business on track towards its ultimate objectives.

To set SMART goals, entrepreneurs can start by conducting a thorough assessment of their business's needs, strengths, and weaknesses. This analysis will inform the identification of key areas that require improvement or growth. By identifying specific areas for development, entrepreneurs can set meaningful goals that address the most critical aspects of their businesses.

Next, entrepreneurs should ensure that their goals are measurable and trackable. Defining key performance indicators (KPIs) allows for the monitoring of progress and the evaluation of success. By regularly reviewing these KPIs, entrepreneurs gain valuable insights into the effectiveness of their strategies and can make adjustments if necessary.

Moreover, entrepreneurs should ensure that their goals are achievable and realistic. Setting unattainable goals can lead to frustration and demotivation. However, this does not mean that goals should be too easy; they should present a challenge that pushes the business to grow but remains within reach with the right amount of effort and resources.

Furthermore, entrepreneurs should strive to keep their goals relevant to both the business and the external environment. Goals should align with market trends, customer demands, and the values of the company. This alignment ensures that the business remains adaptable and responsive to the needs of its stakeholders.

Lastly, entrepreneurs should set deadlines for their goals. By establishing time frames, entrepreneurs create a sense of urgency and prioritize tasks effectively. This time-bound approach helps to maintain focus and prevent goals from being delayed or neglected.

Setting SMART goals is not a one-time activity but an ongoing process. Entrepreneurs should regularly review and revise their goals to reflect the ever-changing business landscape. As circumstances evolve, goals may need to be adjusted or replaced to stay relevant and effective in driving the business forward.

Finally, the concept of setting SMART goals is a fundamental aspect of successful entrepreneurship. By incorporating the qualities of specificity, measurability, achievability, relevance, and time-bound into their goal-setting process, entrepreneurs can create a roadmap that guides their businesses towards growth and prosperity. Through careful analysis and strategic planning, entrepreneurs can align their goals with the vision and mission of their businesses, transforming their ventures from mere dreams to tangible realities.

Creating a Strategic Business Plan

When I wanted to start my agricultural based business, for example, to kick start the process, I embarked on extensive research, delving into countless case studies and examining successful strategies employed by industry giants. I wanted to ensure that my business plan covered all bases and left no room for oversight. It was time to lay the groundwork for my entrepreneurial venture.

Market analysis was the first component on my checklist, and rightfully so. Understanding the market landscape and identifying target customers were crucial elements that would shape the foundation of my business plan. I delved into vast amounts of demographic and psychographic data, exploring the behavior, preferences, and needs of potential customers. Mining through industry reports and surveys, I gained valuable insights into market trends, competitive landscape, and customer demands.

Armed with this knowledge, I moved on to competitive analysis – an essential step in crafting a business plan that would enable my venture to stand out in the crowded marketplace. I meticulously studied my competitors, analyzing their strengths, weaknesses, opportunities, and threats (SWOT Analysis). Identifying areas where my venture could offer unique value propositions was crucial to carve a niche for myself.

With the market and competition analysis laid out, I dove into the financial projections – a narrative that would define the sustainability and growth potential of my future business. This section required a fine balance of realism and optimism, forecasting the revenues, expenses, and profitability of my venture. I had always been comfortable with numbers and had an innate understanding of financial concepts. However, this was my opportunity to display those skills and present a convincing argument to potential investors and stakeholders.

The financial projections section of my business plan was divided into several sub-sections, each addressing specific aspects of my venture's financial strategy. The first step was to estimate startup costs – a meticulous examination of all expenses required to launch the business, from equipment and inventory to employee salaries. I ensured that I accounted for every detail, leaving no room for surprises down the road.

Next, I focused on projecting the revenue streams for my venture. Based on the market analysis and competitive analysis performed earlier, I estimated the potential demand for my product or service and calculated the sales projections. This required a deep understanding of my target market, the price point at which customers would be willing to pay, and the scale at which I anticipated my business to grow.

To enhance the credibility of my financial projections, I also performed a thorough assessment of the industry's growth rate. I reviewed historical data and analyzed market forecasts to determine the projected growth in my sector. This analysis provided me with an understanding of the market's trajectory and allowed me to align my financial projections accordingly.

Additionally, I addressed risks and contingencies in my financial projections, recognizing that unforeseen challenges could arise. I accounted for potential fluctuations in costs, changes in demand, or other market disruptions that could impact my operation. By showcasing my ability to foresee and address these risks, I demonstrated to potential investors that my business plan was solid and well-thought-out.

Throughout the process of creating my strategic business plan, I remained aware of the need for flexibility. Business plans are not set in stone; they adapt and evolve as circumstances change. With this in mind, I made sure that my financial projections allowed room for adjustments, factoring in variables like inflation, interest rates, and even unexpected market opportunities.

Once I had compiled all the necessary information and meticulously revised and refined my business plan, it was time to put it all together into a cohesive document. I strived for clarity, ensuring that my plan was easily understandable and logically organized. I accompanied the written content with visually appealing charts and graphs, illustrating the key data and trends. The overall design aimed to engage and captivate investors, making them confident in the potential of my venture.

Creating a strategic business plan was an arduous process, demanding countless hours of research, analysis, and planning. However, with each step, I felt myself becoming more confident in the path I was forging. Armed with a comprehensive business plan that accounted for all key components, I was ready to take on the world and redeem myself as a successful entrepreneur once again.

Effective Implementation and Execution

Implementing a strategy requires careful planning and attention to detail. It is crucial to have a clear roadmap in place before starting the implementation process. This begins by setting specific goals and objectives that align with the overall vision and mission of your business. By defining these goals, you provide a clear direction for your team, enabling them to understand what needs to be achieved and how their efforts contribute to the overall success.

Once the goals are defined, it is important to break them down into smaller, actionable tasks. This allows for better resource allocation and ensures that each task is manageable and achievable. I have found that creating a detailed project plan with timelines, milestones, and responsibilities assigned to each team member greatly facilitates the implementation process.

However, despite the best-laid plans, challenges are inevitable during the implementation phase. To overcome these challenges, it is essential to maintain open lines of communication and foster a collaborative environment within the team. Regular team meetings and progress updates are essential to address any issues or roadblocks that may arise. Encouraging team members to provide input and share their ideas can also lead to innovative solutions and improvements in the implementation process.

Monitoring progress is another critical aspect of effective implementation and execution. Tracking key performance indicators (KPIs) and regularly reviewing progress against targets allows for early identification of any deviations from the plan. This provides an opportunity to take corrective action and make necessary adjustments before small issues turn into major setbacks. Implementing a robust monitoring system not only ensures accountability but also allows for transparency and visibility into the progress of various tasks and the overall strategy.

Adapting plans as needed is a skill that every successful entrepreneur must possess. The business landscape is constantly changing, and strategies that were effective yesterday may not yield the same results tomorrow. Flexibility and agility are key traits that enable entrepreneurs to adapt to these changes and steer their businesses toward success. Regularly reviewing and revising the strategy based on market trends, customer feedback, and emerging opportunities can help ensure that the implemented strategies remain relevant and effective.

In my own journey, I have encountered numerous challenges during the implementation phase. One such challenge was a lack of clarity and coordination within my team. Despite having a well-defined strategy, there were instances where individual team members were unsure about their roles and responsibilities. To address this, I conducted team-building exercises and implemented a clear communication plan. This not only improved collaboration but also ensured that everyone was on the same page, working towards a common goal.

Another challenge often faced is the resistance to change. As humans, we are naturally resistant to change, and it is no different in a business environment. Implementing new strategies often requires a shift in mindset and breaking away from established routines. To overcome this resistance, you must focus on creating a culture of continuous learning and improvement. You should also encourage your team to embrace change and view it as an opportunity for growth rather than a threat. This shift in perspective will not only make the implementation process smoother but also foster a culture of innovation within the organization.

Throughout the implementation process, it is important to recognize and celebrate small wins. While the ultimate goal may be a long-term vision, acknowledging and celebrating achievements along the way serves as a motivation for the team and boosts morale. It reinforces the idea that their efforts are contributing to the overall success of the business and encourages them to continue striving for excellence.

To cap this, let us understand that effective implementation and execution of strategies are crucial for the success of any business. It is not enough to have brilliant ideas or well-crafted plans. The ability to execute those ideas and plans with precision and adaptability is what sets successful entrepreneurs apart. By setting clear goals, breaking them down into actionable tasks, overcoming implementation challenges, monitoring progress, and adapting plans as needed, entrepreneurs can navigate the ever-changing business landscape, and steer their businesses towards sustainable growth and success.

Risk Management and Contingency Planning

Risk management and contingency planning are crucial components of any successful entrepreneurial journey. As an entrepreneur myself, I have come to realize that taking risks is an inherent part of the game. However, it is the ability to manage and mitigate those risks that separates successful entrepreneurs from the rest.

Throughout my entrepreneurial endeavors, I have faced numerous challenges and uncertainties. From market fluctuations to technological disruptions, the business landscape is fraught with potential pitfalls. It is in the face of these risks that risk management and contingency planning play a critical role in the survival and growth of a business.

To truly understand the importance of risk management, we must first acknowledge that risks can come in different forms and sizes. Some risks are external, such as changes in regulations or economic downturns, while others are internal, like operational inefficiencies or employee turnover. Regardless of their nature, risks can significantly impact the success or failure of a venture.

The first step in risk management is identifying potential risks. This requires a thorough assessment of the business environment and an understanding of the industry dynamics. By analyzing market trends, competitor behavior, and customer preferences, entrepreneurs can identify potential threats and vulnerabilities.

Once risks have been identified, the next step is to evaluate and prioritize them based on their potential impact and likelihood of occurrence. This allows entrepreneurs to focus their resources on managing the most critical risks while considering the constraints of time, money, and expertise.

Mitigating risks is a multi-faceted process that requires a comprehensive approach. One of the most effective strategies is diversification. By diversifying their product offerings or target markets, entrepreneurs can spread their risks and reduce the impact of external factors. Diversification not only provides a safety net but also opens up new opportunities for growth and innovation.

Another important aspect of risk management is the establishment of robust operational procedures. By implementing standardized processes and protocols, entrepreneurs can minimize the risk of human error and operational inefficiencies. This includes ensuring the availability of backup systems and redundancies to handle unexpected events like equipment failure or natural disasters.

Risk management also involves proactive measures to address potential risks before they materialize. This could include securing insurance coverage, entering into legal agreements to protect intellectual property, or establishing effective cyber-security measures. By being proactive, entrepreneurs can significantly reduce the impact of risks on their business.

However, despite all the precautions and proactive measures, unforeseen circumstances can still arise. This is where contingency planning becomes crucial. Contingency planning involves creating backup plans and alternative strategies to handle unexpected situations.

The first step in contingency planning is to identify potential scenarios that could disrupt the normal course of business. This could include a sudden decline in demand, a key supplier going out of business, or the loss of a valuable team member. By considering these potential scenarios, entrepreneurs can develop strategies to mitigate their impact and bounce back quickly.

Contingency plans should consider alternative suppliers, emergency funding sources, and contingency teams. By diversifying suppliers and establishing relationships with multiple vendors, entrepreneurs can reduce the risk of supply chain disruptions. Likewise, having access to emergency funding sources, such as lines of credit or investor partnerships, can provide much-needed financial flexibility during times of crisis.

Furthermore, contingency plans should outline the roles and responsibilities of key team members in the event of unexpected situations. By empowering employees and delegating decision-making authority, entrepreneurs can ensure that the business continues to run smoothly even in their absence.

In addition to these practical measures, entrepreneurs must also cultivate a mindset of adaptability and resilience. The ability to quickly adapt to changing circumstances and learn from failures is what sets successful entrepreneurs apart. By embracing uncertainty and leveraging setbacks as opportunities for growth, entrepreneurs can navigate through challenging times and emerge stronger than ever.

Risk management and contingency planning, although time-consuming and resource-intensive, are indispensable for the long-term success of any entrepreneurial venture. By actively identifying and mitigating risks, and by developing contingency plans to handle unexpected events, entrepreneurs can navigate the unpredictable journey of entrepreneurship with greater confidence and resilience.

Evaluating and Adjusting Strategies

When I started my first business, I had grand visions and ambitious goals. I believed in my product and had a clear plan in mind. However, the reality of the market was far more challenging than I had anticipated. The initial strategies I had devised didn't yield the expected results, and my business was on the brink of failure.

It was during this dark phase that I knew I needed to take a step back and reevaluate my approach. I couldn't afford to be stubborn or cling to my initial plans; I had to be open to change. Understanding the importance of feedback and performance metrics, I sought the opinions of my customers, employees, and advisors.

Listening to those who were directly involved with my business proved invaluable. They provided me with the insight I needed to identify where my strategies were falling short and the areas that required immediate attention. Their feedback became the foundation upon which I built my path to redemption.

Equipped with this feedback, I started analyzing the performance metrics of my business. It became evident that several key indicators were far from satisfactory. The numbers didn't lie; they illuminated the gaps between my expectations and the reality of how my strategies were performing. Armed with this new understanding, I knew I had to make changes.

Adapting my strategies required a combination of boldness and humility. It meant accepting that I hadn't gotten everything right the first time and recognizing the need to learn and grow. It meant pushing beyond my comfort zone and embracing a new way of doing things.

One of the first areas I tackled was marketing. As I analyzed the feedback and performance metrics, it became clear that my marketing approach was ineffective. I hadn't properly identified my target audience, and my messaging wasn't resonating with them. It was time to redefine my marketing strategies.

To develop a more effective marketing approach, I sought out industry research and conducted competitor analysis. I dove deep into understanding my target audience's preferences, needs, and pain points. Armed with this knowledge, I redesigned my marketing messages and channels, tailoring them to address the specific concerns of my ideal customer.

But it wasn't just about revamping my marketing strategies; it was also about reevaluating my overall business strategy. I realized that my initial focus had been too narrow, limiting my growth potential. I needed to expand my product line, diversify my customer base, and explore new market opportunities.

With a renewed sense of purpose, I set out to refine my business model. I conducted a thorough analysis of market trends and identified emerging opportunities within my industry. I needed to identify the gaps in the market and position myself to fill them. This required careful planning and strategic partnerships.

As I adjusted my strategies, I kept a close eye on performance metrics, ensuring that I was creating measurable goals and tracking progress. I analyzed data related to revenue, customer acquisition costs, customer retention rates, and other key performance indicators. Armed with this information, I made data-driven decisions that informed future adjustments and refinements.

It's important to note that evaluating and adjusting strategies isn't a one-time task; it's an ongoing process. Markets are constantly changing, competition evolves, and customer preferences shift. To remain relevant and successful, I had to continually reevaluate and adjust my strategies.

To foster a culture of continuous improvement within my organization, I encouraged my employees to provide feedback and share their ideas. I held regular meetings to discuss performance metrics, brainstorm solutions, and identify areas in need of adjustment. This collaborative approach ensured that everyone in the company felt invested in the process of evaluation and adjustment.

Throughout this process, the importance of data-driven decision-making became crystal clear. I realized that relying on intuition and gut feelings alone wasn't enough. By analyzing and interpreting data, I could make informed choices that were backed by evidence and had a higher probability of success.

Evaluating and adjusting strategies was a transformative journey for me as an entrepreneur. It forced me to confront my weaknesses, challenge my assumptions, and embrace change. It taught me the value of feedback, the power of performance metrics, and the necessity of continuous improvement.

In essence, the process of evaluating and adjusting strategies based on feedback and performance metrics is an essential part of the entrepreneurial journey. It requires a willingness to listen, learn, and adapt. By making data-driven decisions and continuously refining our strategies, we can ensure long-term success and redemption in the ever-changing world of business.

Chapter Seven
Marketing and Branding

*T*he iconic "Got Milk?" campaign, spearheaded by the California Milk Processor Board, offers a profound example of effective marketing. This campaign was a game-changer, successfully driving milk sales by creating a cultural phenomenon that highlighted the importance of having milk.

Understanding Target Audiences

As an entrepreneur, I quickly realized that success in business relies heavily on understanding your target audience. No matter how great your product or service is, if it doesn't meet the needs and desires of your target audience, it will undoubtedly fall flat. We will delve into the world of understanding target audiences, exploring the various techniques and strategies that can be employed to gain a deeper understanding of the people you are trying to reach.

The first concept we explore is market segmentation. Market segmentation involves dividing a market into distinct groups based on various characteristics, such as demographics, behaviors, and preferences. By identifying different segments within your target market, you can create tailored marketing messages and strategies that resonate with each group, increasing your chances of success.

I vividly recall the moment I first learned about market segmentation. It was during a marketing seminar I attended in the early stages of my entrepreneurial journey. The presenter spoke passionately about the power of understanding your audience at a granular level. He emphasized the need to go beyond surface-level demographics and truly get to know the aspirations, pain points, and motivations of your target audience. It was a light-bulb moment for me. I realized that I had been approaching marketing with a one-size-fits-all mentality, failing to truly connect with my audience on a deeper level.

The seminar also introduced me to the concept of buyer personas. Buyer personas are fictional representations of your ideal customers, based on market research and real data. They help you understand your target audience's wants, needs, and preferences in a more detailed and relatable way. Creating buyer personas involves conducting market research, analyzing customer feedback, and gaining insights from data-driven sources.

Armed with this knowledge, I embarked on a journey to create my own buyer personas. I started by collecting data from my existing customer base, conducting surveys, and analyzing online trends in my industry. I wanted to truly understand my audience's motivations and pain points, and how my product could address their specific needs. It was a painstaking process, but the results were worth it.

Through this research, I discovered that my target audience consisted of two distinct segments: young professionals looking for affordable yet fashionable clothing options, and environmentally conscious individuals searching for sustainable fashion alternatives. These groups had different needs and desires, and I realized that my marketing efforts needed to reflect that.

With my buyer personas in hand, I was able to tailor my marketing strategy to each segment. For the young professionals, I focused on highlighting the affordability and trendy styles of my clothing line. For the environmentally conscious individuals, I emphasized the sustainable materials and ethical manufacturing processes behind my products. By speaking directly to the specific needs and desires of each segment, I was able to create a more meaningful connection with my audience, resulting in increased brand loyalty and sales.

But understanding target audiences doesn't stop at market segmentation and buyer personas. It also involves conducting market research to gather valuable insights and identify trends that can inform your marketing strategies. Market research can take various forms, from surveys and focus groups to analyzing industry reports and competitor analysis.

I became almost obsessed with market research, constantly seeking out new data and trends to inform my decision-making process. I devoured industry reports, attended trade shows, and conducted customer interviews to gain a deeper understanding of the market landscape. This research allowed me to stay ahead of the game, anticipate changes in consumer preferences, and craft marketing campaigns that resonated with my target audience.

One particular market research endeavor stands out in my mind. I was in the process of launching a new line of fitness apparel, and I wanted to ensure that my product would meet the needs of my target audience: health-conscious individuals looking for functional yet stylish workout gear. I conducted focus groups, asking participants questions about their workout routines, their pain points with existing workout apparel, and their desired features in new products.

The insights I gained from the focus groups were invaluable. I discovered that comfort and durability were top priorities for my target audience, followed closely by aesthetics and functionality. Armed with this knowledge, I was able to develop a line of garments that not only addressed these needs but exceeded expectations. The line became a hit, and my customer base grew rapidly as a result.

Understanding target audiences and their needs is not a one-time process; it requires ongoing research and analysis. As trends change and new technologies emerge, it is crucial to stay up to date and adapt your marketing strategies accordingly. By investing in understanding your target audience, you are laying the foundation for long-term success and building a loyal customer base that will support your business through thick and thin.

Finally, understanding target audiences is a crucial aspect of running a successful business. Market segmentation, buyer personas, and market research are powerful tools that can help entrepreneurs tailor their marketing strategies to meet the specific needs and desires of their target audience. By investing time and effort into understanding your audience, you can create meaningful connections, drive sales, and ultimately achieve the redemption and success you seek as an entrepreneur.

It is through this journey of understanding target audiences that I learned the true power of connecting with people on a deeper level. Being able to speak directly to their needs and desires has made all the difference in my entrepreneurial endeavors, transforming my business from a bust to a booming success.

Crafting Compelling Marketing Messages

Marketing messages are the cornerstone of any successful business. They are the vehicles through which entrepreneurs communicate their brand value, unique selling propositions, and overall message to potential customers. However, crafting these messages is not an easy task. It requires an in-depth understanding of the target audience, the ability to tell a compelling story, and the skill to evoke the right emotions.

One of the most powerful tools in crafting marketing messages is storytelling. Stories have the ability to capture our attention, engage our emotions, and leave a lasting impact. They create a connection between the brand and the audience, allowing the message to be more memorable and relatable. Through storytelling, entrepreneurs can effectively communicate their brand's values, mission, and purpose.

To craft a compelling marketing message using storytelling, one must start by identifying the target audience. Understanding their needs, desires, and pain points is crucial in creating a story that resonates with them. By delving deep into the audience's psyche, entrepreneurs can uncover the emotional triggers that will capture their attention and persuade them to take action.

Once the audience is identified, entrepreneurs can begin to shape their story. A compelling story has a clear protagonist, conflict, and resolution. It takes the audience on a journey, making them feel a range of emotions and ultimately leading them to a solution provided by the entrepreneur's product or service.

For example, imagine a company that sells eco-friendly cleaning products. Their target audience may be environmentally-conscious individuals who value sustainability and want to reduce their carbon footprint. The company could tell a story of a family struggling with allergies caused by harsh chemical cleaners. They could showcase the family's journey towards a healthier, cleaner home and the impact it has had on their lives. By relating to the audience's desire for a safer, more sustainable living environment, the company can create a compelling marketing message that resonates with their target audience.

Alongside storytelling, emotional appeals play a critical role in crafting compelling marketing messages. Emotions have the power to drive decision-making, and leveraging them in marketing can be highly effective. By tapping into the audience's emotions, entrepreneurs can elicit a response that goes beyond rational thinking and connects with their desires and aspirations.

Different emotions can be evoked depending on the message the entrepreneur wants to convey. For example, to create a sense of urgency, they may use fear or scarcity. To inspire action, they may use excitement or inspiration. By understanding the emotional triggers that resonate with their target audience, entrepreneurs can tailor their marketing messages to elicit the desired response.

Let's go back to the example of the eco-friendly cleaning products company. In their marketing messages, they could tap into the audience's emotions by highlighting the dangers of traditional cleaning products and the potential harm they can cause to human health and the environment.

By evoking fear and concern for the well-being of loved ones, the company can position themselves as the solution to this problem, appealing to the audience's desire for a safer, healthier lifestyle.

Finally, the power of persuasive communication cannot be underestimated in crafting compelling marketing messages. Persuasion is the art of influencing others and driving them towards a specific action. In marketing, it is about convincing potential customers that they need the entrepreneur's product or service and that it is the best choice available.

Effective persuasive communication relies on several key elements. These include establishing credibility, building trust, addressing objections, and providing evidence of the product or service's effectiveness. Entrepreneurs must position themselves as authorities in their field, capable of delivering on their promises. By addressing potential objections and providing evidence, such as testimonials or case studies, entrepreneurs can overcome skepticism and instill confidence in their target audience.

Returning to the eco-friendly cleaning products company, they could use persuasive communication to convince potential customers of the effectiveness and benefits of their products. By sharing success stories of satisfied customers, providing scientific evidence of their products' eco-friendliness, and offering a money-back guarantee, the company can build trust and credibility. They can effectively persuade their target audience that their products are not only safe and sustainable but also highly effective in achieving their cleaning goals.

Crafting compelling marketing messages is a skill that every entrepreneur must master. By understanding the power of storytelling, emotional appeals, and persuasive communication, entrepreneurs can create messages that resonate with their target audience, capture their attention, and ultimately drive them towards taking action. With careful thought, research, and creativity, entrepreneurs can transform their marketing from mediocre to extraordinary, propelling their business The Resilient Entrepreneur.

Building a Strong Brand Identity

When I first started my entrepreneurial journey, I had a vision for my business, but I soon came to realize that a vision alone was not enough to succeed. I needed to build a strong brand identity that would set my business apart from the competition and resonate with my target audience.

This section focuses on the steps and strategies I took to create a brand identity that would become the backbone of my company's success.

To build a strong brand identity, one must first understand the various elements that make up this crucial aspect of a business. Brand values are the guiding principles and beliefs that define what a brand stands for. These values establish the foundation upon which all other brand elements are built. Through extensive research and reflection, I identified the core values that aligned with the mission and purpose of my business. These values not only helped shape my brand identity but also ensured that my decisions and actions were in line with what I wanted my business to represent.

Another essential aspect of brand identity is brand voice. This is the unique personality and tone of voice that a brand uses to communicate with its audience. It is through the brand voice that a business can establish a meaningful connection with its customers. As I developed my brand voice, I took into consideration the preferences and expectations of my target audience. I wanted to ensure that my communication style was relatable and compelling, allowing my audience to feel connected and understood. Consistency in my brand voice across various channels and touch-points was crucial to maintaining a cohesive and recognizable identity.

Visual branding is yet another fundamental element of brand identity. It encompasses the logo, colors, typography, and overall visual design that represents a brand. This visually appealing aspect is often the first thing that catches the audience's attention and leaves a lasting impression. I collaborated with talented designers to create a logo that encapsulated the essence of my brand while keeping it simple and memorable. I carefully selected colors that reflected the personality of my business and evoked the desired emotions in my audience. Typography played a crucial role in establishing the overall aesthetic and readability of my brand. Through meticulous attention to detail, I crafted a visually attractive and cohesive visual branding strategy that aligned with my brand values and communicated the desired message to my audience.

Differentiation is key in today's saturated market. To stand out from the competition, I needed to find unique strategies to differentiate my brand. One of the ways in which I achieved this was by focusing on the storytelling aspect of my brand. I realized that people connect with stories more deeply and emotionally than with mere product features and benefits. I crafted a compelling brand story that resonated with my target audience, using it as a powerful tool to differentiate myself from my competitors. This narrative became the thread that tied together all aspects of my brand identity, from the brand values to the visual branding, creating a cohesive and memorable experience for my customers.

Additionally, I paid close attention to the customer experience my brand provided. Every interaction a customer had with my business, whether it be on the website, through customer service, or in the purchasing process, needed to be consistent with the brand identity I had created. By consistently delivering on my brand promises and providing exceptional customer service, I was able to build a loyal customer base that recognized and valued the unique identity my brand offered. This customer-centric approach not only helped differentiate my brand but also fostered long-term relationships with my customers.

In summary, building a strong brand identity is an essential step in the journey of an entrepreneur. By understanding and incorporating the elements of brand values, brand voice, and visual branding, one can create a unique and memorable brand identity that resonates with the target audience. By differentiating the brand through storytelling and providing a consistent and exceptional customer experience, an entrepreneur can set their business on the path to success. With a strong brand identity as the foundation, my journey The Resilient Entrepreneur became a reality, and I was able to redeem myself as a successful entrepreneur.

Effective Online Marketing Strategies

In today's digital age, online marketing has become an essential component for businesses to not only survive but thrive. The power of the internet has opened up countless opportunities for entrepreneurs to connect with their target audience, increase brand awareness, and drive sales. As an entrepreneur myself, I understand the importance of utilizing effective online marketing strategies to catapult a business into success.

One of the most powerful tools in the digital marketing arsenal is social media. With billions of users worldwide, platforms such as Facebook, Instagram, Twitter, and LinkedIn offer an unparalleled opportunity to connect with potential customers. By leveraging social media, entrepreneurs can engage with their target audience, build relationships, and promote their products or services. The key to using social media effectively is to create compelling and shareable content that resonates with your audience. This content should not only inform and entertain but also provide value to your followers. By consistently providing valuable content, you can position yourself as an expert in your industry, gaining trust and credibility among your target audience.

Another critical online marketing strategy is content marketing. Content is the backbone of any successful digital marketing campaign. By creating and sharing high-quality content, entrepreneurs can establish themselves as industry leaders, attract organic traffic to their website, and generate leads. When it comes to content marketing, it's crucial to understand your target audience and tailor your content to their needs and interests. This requires thorough research and a deep understanding of your audience's pain points and desires. By addressing their challenges and providing solutions through your content, you can attract and retain your target audience, ultimately leading to higher conversions and sales.

Search engine optimization (SEO) is another vital aspect of effective online marketing. When users search for products or services on search engines like Google, you want your website to appear at the top of the search results. This can be achieved through proper SEO techniques, including keyword research, on-page optimization, link building, and technical optimization. By optimizing your website for search engines, you increase its visibility, drive organic traffic, and improve your chances of converting visitors into customers. SEO is an ever-evolving field, and staying updated with the latest trends and algorithms is essential to reaching and maintaining high search engine rankings.

In addition to social media, content marketing, and SEO, entrepreneurs must utilize other digital marketing techniques to maximize their online presence. Pay-per-click (PPC) advertising is an effective way to drive targeted traffic to your website, as you only pay when someone clicks on your ad. Email marketing is another powerful tool that allows you to build a loyal customer base and nurture leads. By sending targeted and personalized emails, entrepreneurs can keep their brand top of mind and drive repeat business. Influencer marketing is also on the rise, allowing entrepreneurs to leverage the influence and reach of popular social media personalities to promote their products or services.

So, effective online marketing strategies are essential for entrepreneurs looking to thrive in today's digital landscape. By utilizing social media, content marketing, SEO, and other digital techniques, entrepreneurs can connect with their target audience, increase brand awareness, and drive sales.

These strategies require a deep understanding of your audience, as well as continuous research and adaptation to stay ahead of the competition. In the fast-paced world of digital marketing, entrepreneurs must be agile and willing to embrace new technologies and trends to gain a competitive edge. With the right online marketing strategies in place, entrepreneurs can transform their businesses The Resilient Entrepreneur, realizing their full potential and achieving their entrepreneurial redemption.

Building Customer Relationships and Loyalty

Building successful relationships with customers is the foundation of any thriving business. In today's competitive landscape, where customers have endless choices and options, it has become more crucial than ever to ensure that they not only choose your brand initially but also remain loyal to it in the long run.

To truly understand the significance of building customer relationships, we need to delve into the historical timeline of business practices. In the early days, when businesses were small and localized, building relationships with customers came naturally. Shopkeepers knew their customers by name, understood their preferences, and provided personalized service. This personal touch went a long way in creating a sense of trust and loyalty between customers and businesses.

However, as businesses began to expand, and globalization took hold, the personalized touch diminished. Corporations were focused on growth and maximizing profits, often neglecting the very customers who were instrumental in their success. This shift in priorities gradually eroded customer relationships, leading to a decrease in loyalty and a rise in consumer skepticism.

Yet, amidst this changing landscape, certain companies understood the paramount importance of nurturing customer relationships. They recognized that loyal customers not only make repeat purchases but also become ambassadors for their brand. It was this realization that led them to develop strategies for exceptional customer experiences, creating brand advocates, and leveraging customer feedback.

Creating exceptional customer experiences involves providing value and exceeding customer expectations at every touch-point. This means ensuring that product quality is top-notch, delivery is prompt and hassle-free, and customer service is outstanding. Every interaction with a customer should be an opportunity to showcase the values and mission of your brand, leaving a lasting positive impression.

One company that stands out in delivering exceptional customer experiences is Zappos. They have built their entire business model around making their customers happy. Zappos not only provides free shipping and hassle-free returns but also goes above and beyond by offering exceptional customer service. Their representatives are trained to actively listen to customer concerns, empathize with their problems, and find appropriate solutions. This commitment to customer satisfaction has resulted in a loyal customer base that not only buys from Zappos but also actively promotes the brand to their friends and family.

Creating brand advocates is another critical aspect of building customer relationships and fostering loyalty. Brand advocates are customers who not only make repeat purchases but also actively promote and recommend the brand to others. These customers become valuable assets as they generate positive word-of-mouth, which can significantly impact the growth and success of a business.

To create brand advocates, businesses must focus on building a strong emotional connection with their customers. This connection goes beyond just selling products; it involves cultivating a genuine relationship based on trust, transparency, and shared values. Coca-Cola, for example, has successfully created brand advocates by associating their brand with happiness, togetherness, and nostalgia. They have crafted marketing campaigns that elicit emotions and create a sense of belonging. As a result, customers not only enjoy their products but also feel a sense of loyalty towards the brand.

In addition to delivering exceptional experiences and creating brand advocates, leveraging customer feedback is crucial in building strong customer relationships. Listening to the needs, wants, and concerns of customers enables businesses to continuously improve their products and services. It also shows customers that their opinions matter, fostering a sense of loyalty and trust.

Collecting customer feedback can be done through various channels, such as surveys, social media engagement, and customer support interactions. Airbnb, for instance, actively seeks feedback from both hosts and guests to continuously enhance their platform and address any issues. By incorporating customer suggestions and making improvements based on their feedback, Airbnb has not only been able to build stronger relationships with their customers but also differentiate themselves from competitors.

As an entrepreneur, I have come to realize the significance of building strong customer relationships and fostering loyalty. In my own journey, I initially focused solely on growth and profitability. However, I soon realized that without the support and loyalty of my customers, my business would not survive in the long run.

Implementing strategies for delivering exceptional customer experiences, creating brand advocates, and leveraging customer feedback has transformed my business. By providing personalized service, going above and beyond to meet customer expectations, and actively seeking their feedback, I have been able to establish a loyal customer base that not only continues to support my business but also acts as brand ambassadors.

It is essential for entrepreneurs and business owners to understand that building customer relationships and fostering loyalty is not an overnight process. It requires dedication, perseverance, and a genuine commitment to providing value to customers. By focusing on delivering exceptional experiences, creating brand advocates, and listening to customer feedback, businesses can turn The Resilient Entrepreneur and secure long-term success in today's competitive market.

Chapter Eight
Financial Management and Growth

W*arren Buffett, renowned as the "Oracle of Omaha," applied a disciplined approach to investing and financial management. His strategy of long-term value investing brought immense growth to Berkshire Hathaway. Buffett's legendary acumen and financial expertise continue to be an inspiration for investors worldwide.*

Financial Planning and Budgeting

Financial planning is the foundation upon which a successful business is built. It involves setting goals and objectives, identifying the necessary resources, and creating a roadmap to achieve those goals. Without a well-defined plan, a business is like a ship without a compass, drifting aimlessly in the vast sea of uncertainty.

The first step in financial planning and budgeting is to develop a comprehensive understanding of the business's revenue streams. This includes analyzing historical data to identify patterns and trends, conducting market research to identify potential new revenue sources, and forecasting future revenue based on market conditions and business strategies. By understanding the company's revenue generation capability, entrepreneurs can make informed decisions about resource allocation and investment opportunities.

One technique that I find particularly useful in forecasting revenue is the bottom-up approach. This involves breaking down revenue projections by individual products or services and analyzing their growth potential. By considering factors such as market demand, competition, and pricing, entrepreneurs can estimate the revenue each product or service is likely to generate. This granular approach provides a more accurate assessment of revenue potential and allows for targeted action plans to be developed to maximize growth.

Managing expenses is another crucial aspect of financial planning. It is not enough to generate revenue; entrepreneurs must also ensure that expenses are kept in check to maintain a healthy profit margin. To do this effectively, entrepreneurs need to implement budgetary controls and regularly review expenses to identify areas where cost savings can be made.

To optimize cash flow, entrepreneurs must carefully manage their working capital. This includes managing accounts receivables, accounts payables, and inventory levels. By implementing effective credit control measures, entrepreneurs can ensure that customers pay on time, reducing the risk of cash flow problems. Similarly, negotiating favorable terms with suppliers can help to extend payment terms and reduce the strain on liquidity.

To gain a complete understanding of the financial health of the business, entrepreneurs should also prepare regular financial statements. These statements, such as the income statement, balance sheet, and cash flow statement, provide insights into the company's financial performance and help identify areas of improvement. By regularly monitoring these statements, entrepreneurs can make informed decisions about resource allocation and identify potential financial risks.

In addition to these techniques, entrepreneurs can also seek the guidance of financial professionals, such as accountants or financial advisors, to ensure that their financial planning is robust and aligned with their business goals. These professionals can provide valuable insights and expertise, helping entrepreneurs to navigate complex financial landscapes and make informed decisions.

Financial planning and budgeting are not one-time activities; they should be an ongoing process that adapts to changing market conditions and business dynamics. Regularly reviewing and updating financial plans is essential to ensure that they remain aligned with the business's strategic objectives. By doing so, entrepreneurs can proactively identify risks and opportunities and make appropriate adjustments to their business strategies.

Therefore, financial planning and budgeting are essential components of successful entrepreneurship. By implementing effective techniques for forecasting revenue, managing expenses, and optimizing cash flow, entrepreneurs can lay a solid foundation for business growth and sustainable success. It is a strategic process that requires careful attention to detail and continuous monitoring and adjustment. By prioritizing financial planning and budgeting, entrepreneurs can navigate the complexities of entrepreneurship with confidence and drive their businesses towards a prosperous future.

Funding Options for Entrepreneurs

When it comes to starting a business, one of the most crucial elements is securing funding. As an entrepreneur, I have experienced the challenges and triumphs associated with finding the right funding strategy firsthand. Here, I'll take you on a journey through the different funding options available, their advantages, disadvantages, and how to determine which one is the right fit for your entrepreneurial endeavors.

Bootstrapping:

The first option to consider is bootstrapping, which involves using personal savings or resources to fund your business. This method offers complete control over the business since you aren't beholden to investors. However, it also requires a significant financial commitment on your part, as you may need to dip into your personal savings or take on additional jobs to support your business. Bootstrapping can be a viable option for entrepreneurs who have a solid financial foundation and want to maintain full control over their vision.

Loans:

Another funding option is taking out a loan, which allows you to borrow a specific amount of money that must be repaid within a defined timeframe, usually with interest. Loans can be obtained from banks, credit unions, or even online lenders. This approach provides immediate access to capital but comes with the burden of repayment, including interest charges. It's essential to carefully consider the terms and conditions of the loan, ensuring that the repayment schedule aligns with your business's projected cash flow. Taking on debt can be a viable option for entrepreneurs who have a clear plan for generating revenue and are confident in their ability to repay the loan.

Venture Capital:

For those looking to scale their business quickly, venture capital might be the funding option to explore. Venture capital involves raising funds from investors who provide capital in exchange for equity or ownership in the company. This option can provide substantial capital and mentorship from experienced investors who can help accelerate your business's growth. However, it also means diluting your ownership and giving up some control. Venture capital is best suited for entrepreneurs with high-growth potential and a strong, scalable business model.

Crowd-Funding:

Finally, crowd-funding has gained significant popularity as a funding option in recent years. It involves raising funds from a large number of people, typically through online platforms.

Crowd-funding allows entrepreneurs to tap into a wide network of potential investors who are interested in supporting innovative ideas. This option offers not only financial support but also a way to validate your business concept and build a community of early adopters. However, it requires a well-thought-out marketing strategy to capture the attention and interest of potential investors. Crowd-funding is a viable option for entrepreneurs looking to test the market demand for their product or service and engage with potential customers.

The Pros and Cons

Now that we have explored the different funding options, it's essential to consider their pros and cons to make an informed decision.

Bootstrapping provides control, but it can also limit growth potential due to limited resources.

Loans offer immediate access to capital, but the burden of repayment can negatively impact cash flow.

Venture capital offers substantial funding and expertise, but it comes with the loss of ownership and control.

Crowd-funding provides a platform for marketing and validating your idea, but it requires a well-executed campaign to be successful.

Considering these factors will help you decide which funding option aligns best with your business goals, growth plans, and risk tolerance.

Determining the right funding strategy for your entrepreneurial journey is no easy task. It requires careful evaluation of your financial situation, business goals, and growth potential. It's important to explore all available options, weigh their pros and cons, and consider how they align with your long-term vision. Additionally, seeking advice from mentors, industry experts, and other successful entrepreneurs who have been through the funding process can provide invaluable insights and guidance.

Remember, funding is just one piece of the puzzle when it comes to building a successful business. It is crucial to have a solid business plan, a clear understanding of your target market, and a strong value proposition. Ultimately, your dedication, perseverance, and ability to adapt to market conditions will play a significant role in your entrepreneurial success.

Managing Business Finances

Bookkeeping forms the foundation of efficient financial management. It involves keeping track of all financial transactions and recording them accurately. In the early stages of my entrepreneurial journey, this aspect of business finance often overwhelmed me. However, I soon realized that maintaining accurate books not only helped me understand my business's financial health but also enabled me to make informed decisions about investments, expansion, and cost-cutting measures.

To streamline my bookkeeping process, I adopted an organized approach. I diligently recorded every expense and revenue in a ledger, categorizing them appropriately. This enabled me to generate financial reports regularly and assess the profitability of my business. The process also made tax season less daunting, as I had all the necessary information to prepare my tax returns in an organized manner.

Financial statements are crucial tools for assessing a business's financial standing, and they play a pivotal role in attracting investors and securing loans. I dedicated time to understanding the different components of financial statements, such as the balance sheet, income statement, and cash flow statement. These statements provided me with insights into the overall financial health of my business, highlighting areas of strength and areas that required attention.

The balance sheet revealed the company's assets, liabilities, and shareholders' equity, offering a snapshot of its financial position at a specific point in time. Armed with this knowledge, I was able to make informed decisions regarding risk management and capital allocation. The income statement, on the other hand, summarizes the company's revenues, expenses, and net income or loss. Analyzing this statement allowed me to assess the profitability of my business and identify areas where expenses could be reduced or revenue streams enhanced.

The cash flow statement was another invaluable tool in managing my business's finances. It provided a detailed account of the inflow and outflow of cash, allowing me to anticipate and address any potential cash flow problems. By monitoring my cash flow regularly, I could ensure that I had enough liquid assets to cover operational expenses, invest in growth opportunities, and withstand any unexpected financial challenges that may arise.

Tax planning was an area that initially seemed overwhelming. However, by taking proactive steps and seeking professional advice, I was able to navigate through the complexities of tax regulations and maximize my tax savings. Proper tax planning not only ensured compliance with the law but also helped me optimize my business's financial performance.

I realized that hiring the right tax professional was instrumental in minimizing tax liabilities and avoiding costly mistakes. They helped me identify eligible deductions, tax credits, and incentives specific to my industry. By staying up to date with tax laws and regulations, I was able to make informed decisions that positively impacted my business's bottom line.

Compliance with financial regulations is critical for maintaining the trust of stakeholders and avoiding legal repercussions. This involves adhering to various financial reporting requirements, such as filing annual reports, submitting tax returns, and complying with auditing standards. By staying organized and staying ahead of deadlines, I ensured that my business remained in good standing and complied with all necessary regulations.

Furthermore, I recognized the importance of having robust internal controls to safeguard my business's assets, prevent fraud, and maintain the accuracy of financial statements. Implementing segregation of duties and regular internal audits helped me identify any weaknesses in my financial management processes and allowed me to take corrective action promptly.

To wrap this up, it is good to note that managing business finances encompasses a wide range of tasks, from bookkeeping to compliance with financial regulations. By adopting an organized approach to financial management and seeking professional advice when needed, I was able to navigate the intricacies of business finance and secure the long-term success of my entrepreneurial endeavor. Understanding the importance of accurate bookkeeping, financial statements, tax planning, and compliance helped me make informed decisions, attract investors, and ensure the financial stability of my business. By taking control of my business's finances, I was able to transform a struggling venture into a thriving enterprise.

Strategies for Sustainable Growth

The path to success in the world of entrepreneurship is never a smooth one. It is much like a roller coaster ride, with its ups and downs, twists and turns. As an entrepreneur, I had experienced my fair share of setbacks and failures. But rather than letting these obstacles deter me, I embraced them as valuable learning opportunities. It was during one of these challenging times that I realized the importance of implementing sustainable strategies for business growth.

Now let us explore various strategies for achieving sustainable business growth. These strategies are the result of years of research, trial and error, and lessons learned from successful entrepreneurs who have gone The Resilient Entrepreneur. Through extensive interviews, case studies, and personal experiences, I have discovered that there are several key factors that contribute to sustainable growth.

Market Expansion:

The first strategy for sustainable growth is market expansion. In order to grow and thrive in the ever-changing business landscape, it is essential to continually explore new markets and customer segments. This can be achieved through market research and analysis to identify untapped opportunities. By understanding customer needs and preferences, businesses can tailor their products or services to meet these demands and expand their reach.

However, market expansion requires careful planning and execution. It is crucial to assess the feasibility and profitability of entering a new market, as well as the potential risks and challenges. A thorough understanding of the competitive landscape and the target market's demographics, trends, and consumer behavior is essential. Armed with this knowledge, entrepreneurs can develop effective marketing strategies and adapt their products or services to successfully penetrate and capture new markets.

Product Diversification:

Another strategy for sustainable growth is product diversification. In a rapidly changing business environment, it is important to constantly innovate and offer new products or services to meet evolving customer needs. By diversifying their product portfolio, entrepreneurs can not only attract new customers but also retain existing ones.

To effectively diversify their offerings, entrepreneurs must conduct in-depth market research to identify emerging trends and consumer preferences. By understanding the market demand and gaps, entrepreneurs can develop new products that have a competitive advantage. This might involve collaboration with technology partners or conducting extensive research and development to create innovative solutions.

Strategic Partnerships:

Strategic partnerships can also play a vital role in achieving sustainable growth. By forming alliances with complementary businesses or industry leaders, entrepreneurs can leverage their partner's expertise, resources, and customer base. This allows for shared knowledge, increased market visibility, and accelerated growth.

When entering into strategic partnerships, entrepreneurs should carefully evaluate potential partners to ensure compatibility in terms of values, goals, and market positioning. Collaborative agreements, such as joint ventures, licensing agreements, or co-marketing initiatives, can provide access to new markets, distribution channels, and technology.

Scaling Operations:

Scaling operations is a critical aspect of sustainable growth. As demand for products or services increases, entrepreneurs must ensure that their operations can support this growth without compromising product quality or customer satisfaction. Effective scaling requires strategic planning, investment in infrastructure, and the implementation of efficient processes.

To scale operations successfully, entrepreneurs must identify and address any operational bottlenecks or inefficiencies. This could involve streamlining production processes, investing in technology, or hiring and training additional staff. It is crucial to strike a balance between maintaining profitability and meeting increased demand. Continuous monitoring and adjustment of operations are necessary to ensure sustainable growth.

Maintaining Profitability:

While growth is vital, it is equally important to maintain profitability. Achieving sustainable growth requires careful financial management and a focus on long-term profitability rather than short-term gains. Entrepreneurs must set clear financial goals, monitor key performance indicators, and regularly evaluate their business's financial health.

To maintain profitability, entrepreneurs must focus on cost control, optimize pricing strategies, and effectively manage cash flow. This requires regular financial analysis, forecasting, and adherence to budgetary goals. Entrepreneurs should also explore opportunities to increase revenue streams through upselling, cross-selling, or innovative pricing models.

Financial Metrics and Performance Evaluation

Growing a successful business requires more than just a great idea or a fantastic product. It requires constantly monitoring and assessing various aspects of the business to ensure its sustainability. Financial metrics provide invaluable insights into the overall health of a venture, allowing entrepreneurs to identify strengths, weaknesses, and areas for improvement. By understanding financial metrics and performance evaluation, entrepreneurs can make informed decisions that drive growth and profitability.

One of the primary tools for evaluating business performance is key performance indicators (KPIs). KPIs are quantifiable measurements used to assess the achievement of specific objectives. These objectives can vary depending on the industry and the goals of the entrepreneur. However, the ultimate goal of using KPIs is to gain a holistic understanding of the business's performance and identify areas that need improvement.

When it comes to financial metrics and performance evaluation, there is a wide range of KPIs that entrepreneurs can track. Some commonly used financial KPIs include revenue growth rate, gross profit margin, net profit margin, return on investment (ROI), and cash flow. Each of these KPIs provides unique insights into the financial health of the business. For example, revenue growth rate indicates the rate at which the business is growing, while gross profit margin shows the percentage of revenue left after deducting the cost of goods sold. Net profit margin measures the profitability of the business after taking into account all expenses, while ROI indicates the return generated on the investment made in the business. Lastly, cash flow measures the cash inflows and outflows of the business, allowing entrepreneurs to assess their ability to meet financial obligations.

In addition to financial KPIs, entrepreneurs should also consider using non-financial KPIs to evaluate business performance. These non-financial

KPIs are measures that are not directly tied to the financial aspects of the business but still provide valuable insights into overall performance. Examples of non-financial KPIs include customer satisfaction ratings, employee turnover rates, and market share. These KPIs allow entrepreneurs to assess the effectiveness of their marketing and customer service efforts and evaluate the impact on the business's overall growth and success.

While understanding and tracking KPIs is crucial, entrepreneurs must also be equipped with the right financial ratios to evaluate business performance effectively. Financial ratios are mathematical calculations that provide insights into various aspects of the business's financial health. These ratios help entrepreneurs assess liquidity, profitability, efficiency, and solvency.

One essential financial ratio is the current ratio, which compares a business's current assets to its current liabilities. This ratio indicates the business's ability to pay off its short-term obligations. A higher current ratio suggests a stronger financial position and liquidity. Another important ratio is the return on equity (ROE), which measures the profitability of the business by comparing the net income to the shareholders' equity. A higher ROE signifies a more efficient use of shareholders' investments and better profitability.

To further analyze the efficiency of the business's operations, entrepreneurs can calculate the inventory turnover ratio, which measures how quickly the business sells its inventory. A higher inventory turnover ratio indicates that the business is efficiently managing its inventory and generating sales. Additionally, the debt-to-equity ratio measures the proportion of debt and equity financing in the business. A higher debt-to-equity ratio suggests higher financial risk and less equity investment in the business.

To measure and monitor business performance effectively, entrepreneurs should utilize a combination of financial metrics, KPIs, and financial ratios.

These tools provide a comprehensive understanding of the business's financial health, allowing entrepreneurs to make informed decisions.

In terms of methods for measuring and monitoring business performance, there are several approaches entrepreneurs can employ. Firstly, trend analysis involves comparing financial metrics and ratios over time to identify patterns and trends. By analyzing these trends, entrepreneurs can predict future performance and make necessary adjustments to achieve their business goals.

Another method is benchmarking, which involves comparing the business's financial metrics and performance against industry standards or competitors. Benchmarking provides entrepreneurs with a clear picture of where they stand in relation to their peers and helps identify areas for improvement.

Financial forecasting is another valuable method for measuring and monitoring business performance. By using historical financial data and market trends, entrepreneurs can predict future financial performance and plan accordingly. Financial forecasting allows entrepreneurs to allocate resources effectively, identify potential risks, and make informed business decisions.

Overall, understanding financial metrics and performance evaluation is essential for entrepreneurs. By utilizing key performance indicators, financial ratios, and various methods for measuring and monitoring business performance, entrepreneurs can ensure the success and sustainability of their ventures. The ability to track and evaluate financial metrics provides insights into the business's overall health, identifies strengths and weaknesses, and enables informed decision-making. As an entrepreneur, I have witnessed firsthand the tremendous benefits of utilizing financial metrics and performance evaluation, and I encourage fellow entrepreneurs to embrace these practices for their own journey of redemption and success.

Conclusion

Rising Strong: From Starting To Finishing Strong

When I think back to the early days of my entrepreneurial journey, I am reminded of the passion and excitement that fueled my drive to pursue my dreams. I had a vision, a goal, and an unwavering belief in my abilities. But as with any journey, there were obstacles along the way. The first setback came sooner than expected. The initial boom quickly turned to bust as unforeseen challenges arose. It was a heartbreaking experience, watching my dreams crumble before my eyes. I questioned my choices, my abilities, and even my worth as an entrepreneur. The fall was hard, but it was not the end.

From that dark moment of defeat, a seed of hope sprouted within me. I realized that failure was not the end, but rather an opportunity to learn and grow. And so, I picked myself up, dusted off the remnants of my shattered dreams, and started anew. I armed myself with determination, resilience, and the invaluable lessons I had learned from my past mistakes. It was a slow and arduous climb, but with each step, I could feel my strength growing and my passion reigniting.

Starting again from scratch was a humbling experience. I had to rebuild not only my business but also my confidence. I sought guidance from mentors who had risen from their own ashes, who had experienced the pain of failure and emerged stronger than ever. Their stories resonated with me, fueling my belief that I too could turn my bust into a boom. Their encouragement and wisdom became my guiding light, reminding me that success was not a destination but a journey, with peaks and valleys, triumphs and setbacks.

As I immersed myself in the process of starting over, I discovered a newfound appreciation for the journey itself. The struggle, the setbacks, and the challenges shaped me into a stronger and more resilient entrepreneur. I learned to embrace failure as a stepping stone towards success, understanding that it was through these experiences that I would gain the necessary insights and skills for future endeavors. Every setback became an opportunity for growth, a chance to learn valuable lessons that would propel me forward. I was no longer afraid of failure; I saw it as an integral part of the journey towards success.

And so, I persevered. I pushed through the tough times, pivoted when necessary, and adapted to the ever-changing business landscape. Slowly but surely, my business began to thrive again. The boom that I had once experienced in the early days was returning, but this time with a newfound sense of gratitude and resilience. The bust was no longer a source of shame but a testament to my courage and determination. It was through the fall that I discovered my true strength, my unwavering commitment to my dreams.

But the story does not end here. The journey from starting to finishing strong is not simply about reaching a pinnacle of success; it is about continually pushing ourselves to new heights and embracing the challenges that come with growth. Even as my business thrives, I am always aware that complacency is the enemy of progress. I continually seek opportunities to innovate, evolve, and adapt. The entrepreneurial journey is not a linear one; it is a constant cycle of falling, rising, and striving for excellence.

The key to rising strong lies in our ability to harness the lessons of failure, to find the strength within ourselves to rise again. It requires perseverance, courage, and an unwavering belief in our own abilities. The journey The Resilient Entrepreneur is not an easy one, but it is also not unattainable. It is a journey that demands resilience, passion, and a never-ending hunger for growth.

For those entrepreneurs who have fallen, I want you to know that you are not alone. We have all faced moments of defeat, doubt, and uncertainty. But it is in these moments that our true strength and potential lie dormant, waiting to be awakened.

Remember that falling is not failure. It's merely a temporary setback, a stepping stone on the path to success. The stories of those who faced adversity and rebounded, like Oprah Winfrey, Richard Branson, and countless others, are a testament to the indomitable spirit of the entrepreneur. Embrace the fall, learn from it, and gather the courage to rise again. Believe in yourself, for your past does not define your future.

And for those just starting out on their entrepreneurial journey, be strong. The road ahead may be filled with obstacles and setbacks, but know that the challenges you face will shape you into the resilient and successful entrepreneur you are meant to be.

Elon Musk's story is a reminder that audacious visions can change the world. Just as Steve Jobs reinvented Apple, you too can reinvent your future. The journey of the resilient entrepreneur is a cycle of renewal and transformation. Embrace the process, learn from every experience, and never lose sight of your dreams. Success may not come overnight, but with determination and perseverance, your boom is waiting just around the corner.

In conclusion, the journey of the entrepreneur is one fraught with challenges, setbacks, and moments of doubt. But it is also a journey filled with moments of triumph, growth, and unyielding determination. The Resilient Entrepreneur, from starting to finishing strong, the entrepreneurial path is a testament to the power of resilience, the ability to rise again and again.

Remember that the entrepreneurial spirit is not bound by circumstance or age. It is a force that transcends setbacks, a beacon of hope that guides us through uncertainty. No matter where you are in your journey, whether you've stumbled or are just taking your first steps, the potential for success lies within you.

It's time to rise strong, to embrace the challenges, and to continue building, innovating, and growing. The entrepreneurial path is a testament to the human spirit's capacity to endure, adapt, and triumph.

Embrace failure, learn from it, and use it as a catalyst for growth. It is through these experiences that we find our true strength and discover the immense potential within ourselves. So, to all the entrepreneurs out there, whether you have fallen or are just starting out, I urge you to rise strong, embrace the journey, and never lose sight of the extraordinary things you are capable of achieving.

Peace!

www.ingramcontent.com/pod-product-compliance
Lightning Source LLC
Chambersburg PA
CBHW072052230526
45479CB00010B/684